Knowledge Representation 2.0

--The Structure-Behavior Coalescence Approach--

William S. Chao

Structure-Behavior Coalescence

Systems Architecture = Systems Structure + Systems Behavior

CONTENTS

PREFACE

Knowledge representation incorporates findings from psychology about how human beings solve problems and represent knowledge in order to achieve formalisms that will make complex systems easier to construct and build. Knowledge representation also incorporates findings from logic to automate various kinds of reasoning, such as the application of rules or the relations of sets and subsets.

A system has been formalized, by knowledge representation 1.0, hopefully to be an integrated whole, embodied in its assembled components, their interactions with each other and the environment. Since systems structure and systems behavior are the two most prominent views of a system, integrating the systems structure and systems behavior apparently is the best way to achieve a truly integrated whole of a system. Since knowledge representation 1.0 does not describe and represent the integration of systems structure and systems behavior, very likely it will never be able to actually form an integrated whole of a system.

Structure-behavior coalescence (SBC) provides an elegant way to integrate the systems structure and systems behavior, and hence achieves a truly integrated whole, of a system. A truly integrated whole sets a path to achieve the desired knowledge representation. SBC facilitates an integrated whole. Therefore, we conclude that knowledge representation 2.0 using the SBC approach, which contains three fundamental diagrams: a) framework diagram, b) component operation diagram and c) interaction flow diagram, is highly adequate in describing and representing a system.

ABOUT THE AUTHOR

Dr. William S. Chao is the CEO & founder of SBC Architecture International®. SBC (Structure-Behavior Coalescence) architecture is a systems architecture which demands the integration of systems structure and systems behavior of a system. SBC architecture applies to hardware architecture, software architecture, enterprise architecture, knowledge architecture and thinking architecture. The core theme of SBC architecture is: Architecture = Structure + Behavior.

William S. Chao received his bachelor degree (1976) in telecommunication engineering and master degree (1981) in information engineering, both from the National Chiao-Tung University, Taiwan. From 1976 till 1983, he worked as an engineer at Chung-Hwa Telecommunication Company, Taiwan.

William S. Chao received his master degree (1985) in information science and Ph.D. degree (1988) in information science, both from the University of Alabama at Birmingham, USA. From 1988 till 1991, he worked as a computer scientist at GE Research and Development Center, Schenectady, New York, USA.

PART I: BASIC CONCEPTS

Chapter 1: Introduction to Knowledge Representation

Knowledge representation (knowledge architecture) is the field of artificial intelligence that focuses on formalizing computer representations that capture information about the world that can be used to solve complex problems. Knowledge representation (KR) incorporates findings from psychology about how human beings solve problems and represent knowledge in order to achieve formalisms that will make complex systems easier to construct and build. Knowledge representation also incorporates findings from logic to automate various kinds of reasoning, such as the application of rules or the relations of sets and subsets.

The justification for knowledge representation is that conventional procedural code is not the best formalism to use to solve complex problems. Knowledge representation makes complex systems easier to define and maintain than procedural code and can be used in expert systems. For example, talking to experts in terms of business rules rather than code lessens the semantic gap between users and developers and makes development of complex systems more practical.

Knowledge representation goes hand in hand with automated reasoning because one of the main purposes of explicitly describing and representing knowledge is to be able to reason about that knowledge, to make inferences, assert new knowledge, etc. Virtually all knowledge representation languages have a reasoning or inference engine as part of the system.

Multiple views non-integrated approaches for knowledge representation 1.0 include semantics networks, frame languages, first-order logic and lambda calculus. Each of these approaches, more or less, fails to describe and represent a system as an integrated whole of that system's multiple views.

On the contrary, multiple views integrated approaches for knowledge representation 2.0 describe and represent a system as an integrated whole of that system's multiple views..

1-1 Multiple Views of a System

In general, a system is extremely complex that it consists of multiple views such as structure view, behavior view, function view, data view as shown in Figure 1-1 [Denn08, Kend10, Pres09, Somm06].

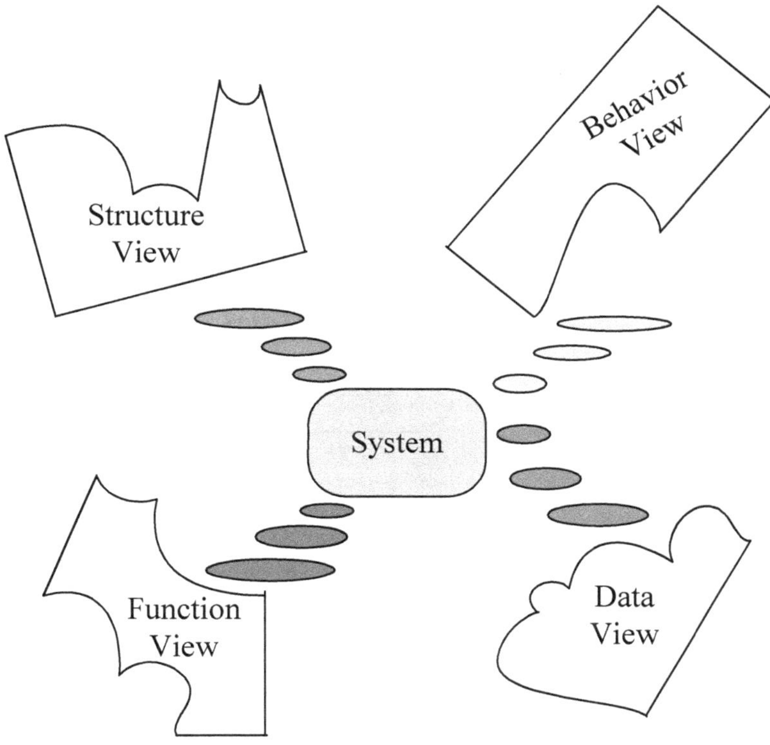

Figure 1-1 Multiple Views of a System

Among the above multiple views, the structure and behavior views are perceived as the two prominent ones. The structure view focuses on the systems structure which is described by components and their composition while the behavior view concentrates on the systems behavior which involves interactions [Chao15a, Chao15b, Chao15c, Chao15d, Chao15e, Hoar85, Miln89, Miln99] among the external environment's actors and components. Function and data views are considered to be other views as shown in Figure 1-2.

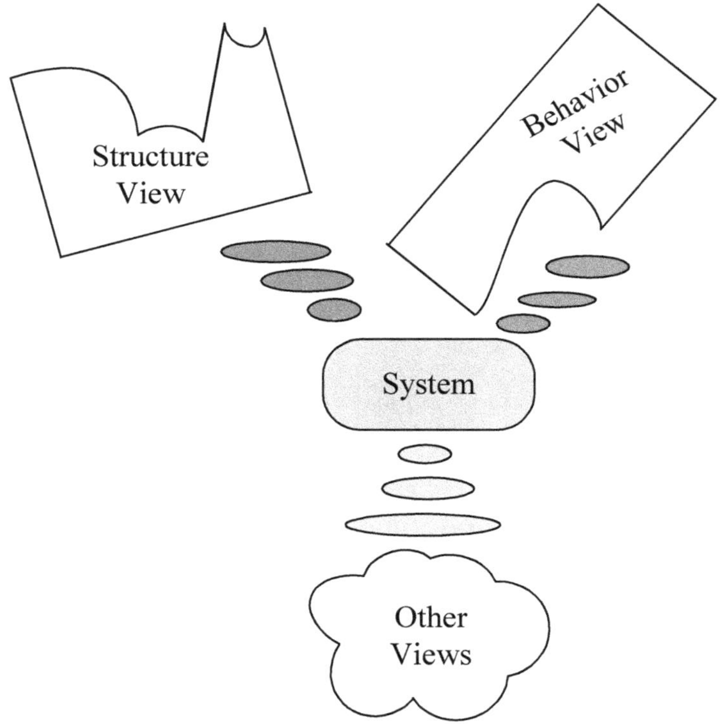

Figure 1-2 Structure, Behavior and Other Views

Either Figure 1-1 or Figure 1-2 represents the multiple views of a system. In some situations Figure 1-1 is used and in other situations Figure 1-2 is used.

Accordingly, a system is described and represented in Figure 1-3 to be an integrated whole of that system's multiple views, i.e., structure, behavior and other views, embodied in its assembled components, their interactions [Chao15a, Chao15b, Chao15c, Chao15d, Chao15e, Hoar85, Miln89, Miln99] with each other and the environment. Components are sometimes labeled as non-aggregated systems, parts, entities, objects and building blocks [Chao14a, Chao14b, Chao14c].

A system is an integrated whole of that system's multiple views, i.e., structure, behavior, and other views, embodied in its assembled components, their interactions with each other and the environment.

Figure 1-3 Description and Representation of a System

Since multiple views are embodied in a system's assembled components which belong to the systems structure, they shall not exist alone. Multiple views must be loaded on the systems structure just like a cargo is loaded on a ship as shown in Figure 1-4. There will be no multiple views if there is no systems structure. Stand-alone multiple views are not meaningful.

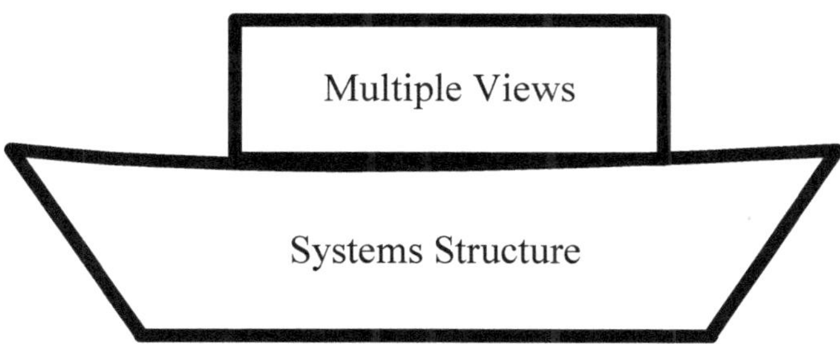

Figure 1-4 Multiple Views Loaded on the Systems Structure

1-2 Multiple Views Non-Integrated Approaches for Knowledge Representation 1.0

When describing and representing a system, the multiple views non-integrated approach, also known as the model multiplicity approach [Dori95, Dori02, Dori16], respectively picks a model for each view as shown in Figure 1-5, the structure view has the structure model; the behavior view has the behavior model; the function view has the function model; the data view has the data model. These multiple models, are heterogeneous and not related to each other, and thus become the primary cause of model multiplicity problems [Dori95, Dori02, Dori16, Pele02, Sode03].

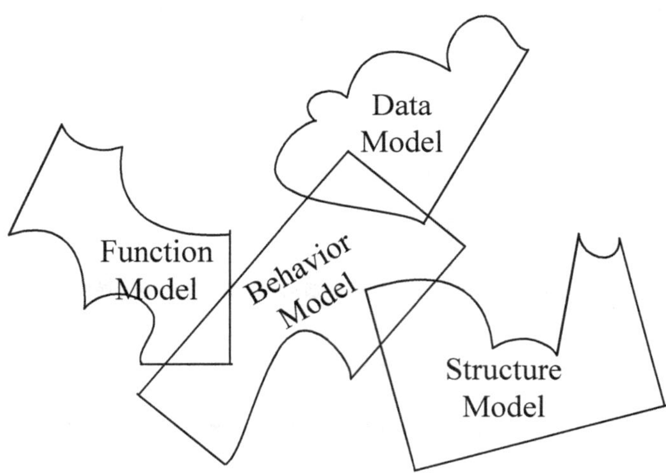

Figure 1-5 Multiple Views Non-Integrated Approach

Multiple views non-integrated approaches for knowledge representation 1.0 fall into four general categories: functional-based (*Lisp*, *Lambda Calculus*) [Mich11], frame-based (*Frame Languages*) [Mins74], logic-based (*First-Order Logic*, *Prolog*) [Smul95] and data structure-based (*Semantics Networks*) [Sowa91], as shown in Figure 1-6. Each of these approaches, more or less, fails to describe and represent a system as an integrated whole of that system's multiple views.

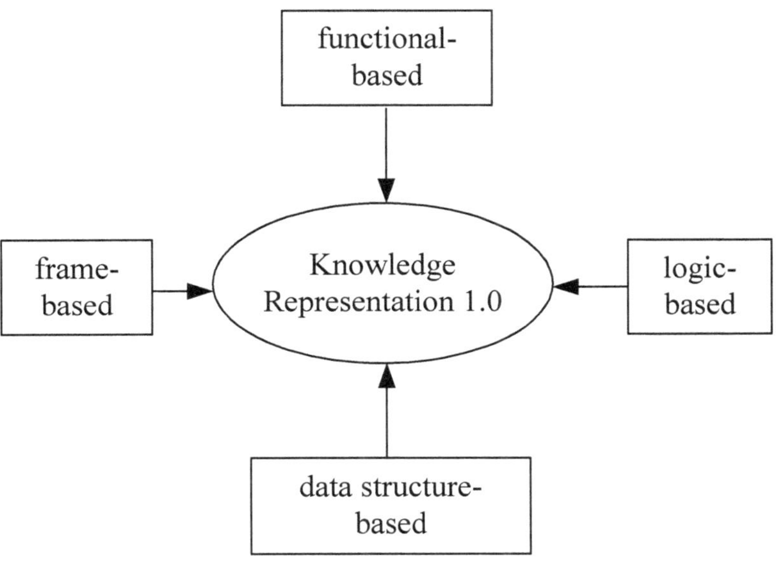

Figure 1-6 Multiple Views Non-Integrated Approaches for Knowledge Representation 1.0

1-3 Multiple Views Integrated Approaches for Knowledge Representation 2.0

When describing and representing a system, the multiple views integrated approach, also known as the model singularity approach

[Dori95, Dori02, Dori16, Pele02, Sode03], instead of picking many heterogeneous and unrelated models, will use only one single model as shown in Figure 1-7. The structure, behavior, function and data views are all integrated in this one single model which represents an integrated whole of that system's multiple views [Chao14a, Chao14b, Chao14c].

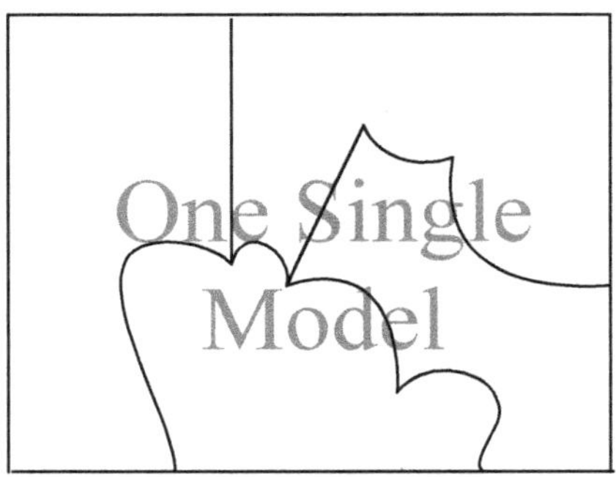

Figure 1-7 Multiple Views Integrated Approach

Multiple views integrated approaches for knowledge representation 2.0 describe and represent a system as an integrated whole of that system's multiple views.

Chapter 2: Systems Structure and Systems Behavior

Systems structure and systems behavior are the two most significant views of a system. Systems structure, described and represented by components and their operations and their composition, refers to the type of connection between the components of a system. Systems behavior, described and represented by the interactions between and among the components and environment, refers to the interconnectivities a system in conjunction with its environment.

2-1 Structure of Systems

Every system forms a whole. In general, structure of systems is the type of connection between the components of a system. More specifically, we describe and represent the structure of a system by 1) components, 2) their operations and 3) their composition.

Components are something relatively indivisible in a system [Hoff10, Shel11]. For example, *MTPDS_GUI*, *Age_Logic*, *Overweight_Logic* and *Personal_Database* are components of the *Multi-Tier Personal Data System* as shown in Figure 2-1.

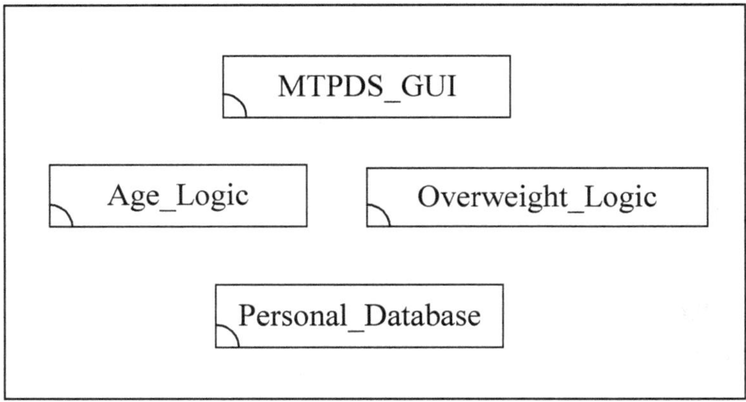

Figure 2-1 Components of the *Multi-Tier Personal Data System*

An operation provided by each component represents a procedure or method or function of the component [Chao14a, Chao14b, Chao14c]. Each component in a system must possess at least one operation. Figure 2-2 shows the operations of all components of the *Multi-Tier Personal Data System*. In the figure, component *MTPDS_GUI* has two operations: *Calculate_AgeClick* and *Calculate_OverweightClick*; component *Age_Logic* has one operation: *Calculate_Age*; component *Overweight_Logic* has one operation: *Calculate_Overweight*; component *Personal_Database* has two operations: *Sql_DateOfBirth_Select* and *Sql_SexHeightWeight_Select*.

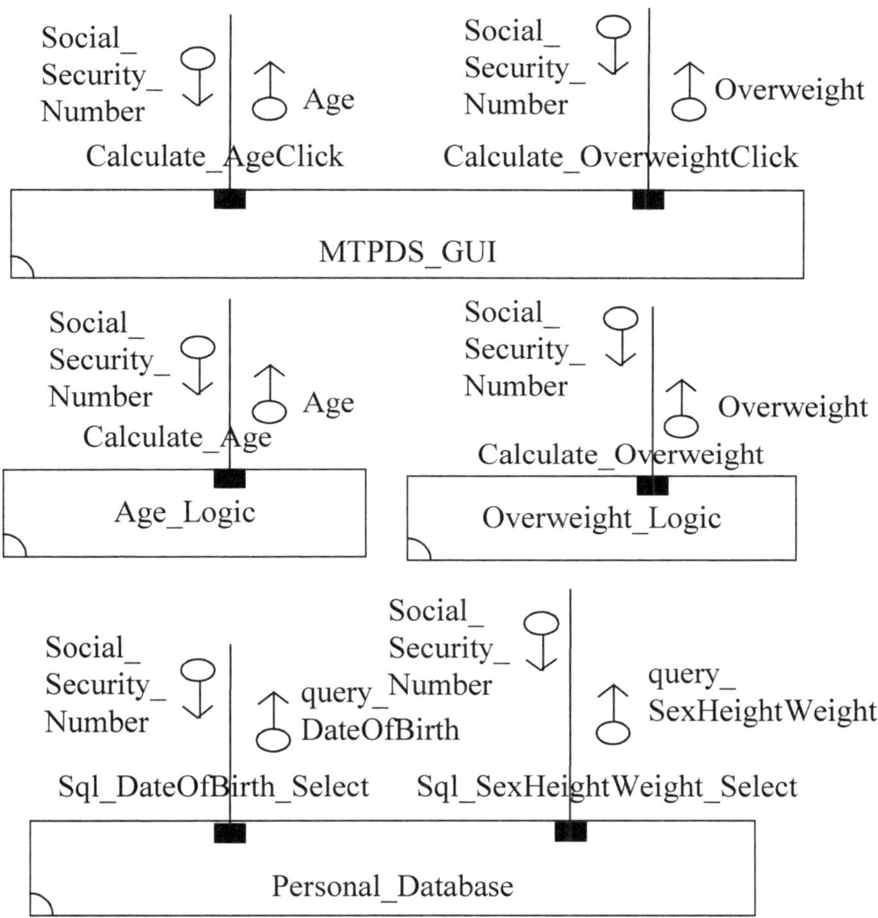

Figure 2-2 Operations of all Components of the *Multi-Tier Personal Data System*

Composition of components describes and represents the structural composition and decomposition of a system. For example, Figure 2-3 shows that, in the *Multi-Tier Personal Data System*, *Presentation_Layer* contains the *MTPDS_GUI* component; *Logic_Layer* contains the

Age_Logic and *Overweight_Logic* components; *Data_Layer* contains the *Personal_Database* component.

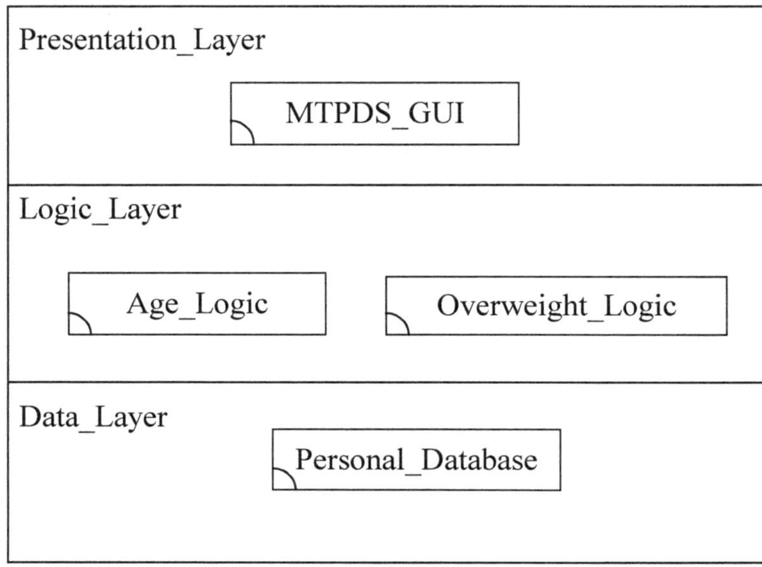

Figure 2-3 Structural Composition of the *Multi-Tier Personal Data System*

2-2 Behavior of Systems

Systems behavior refers to the interactions a system in conjunction with its environment. It is the response of a e system to various stimuli, whether internal or external, conscious or subconscious, overt or covert, and voluntary or involuntary.

For example, Figure 2-4 demonstrates two individual behaviors: *AgeCalculation* and *OverweightCalculation* that refer to the interactions the *Multi-Tier Personal Data System* in conjunction with its environment.

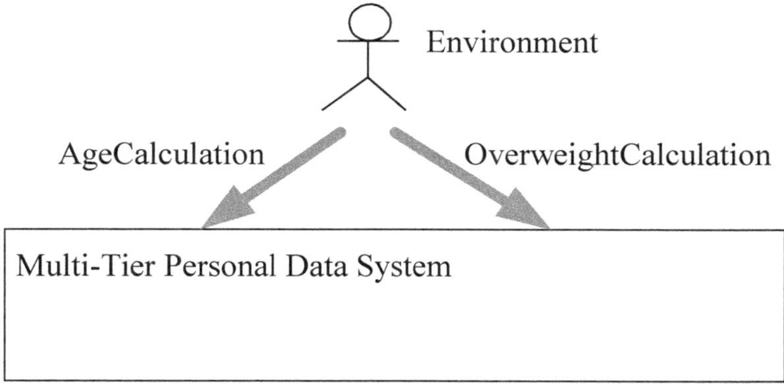

Figure 2-4 Behaviors of the *Multi-Tier Personal Data System*

For each behavior, the environment always initiates the interaction and will lead more follow-up interactions to be realized among components. For example, Figure 2-5 demonstrates that interactions between and among the environment and the *MTPDS_GUI*, *Age_Logic* and *Personal_Database* components shall draw forth the *AgeCalculation* behavior.

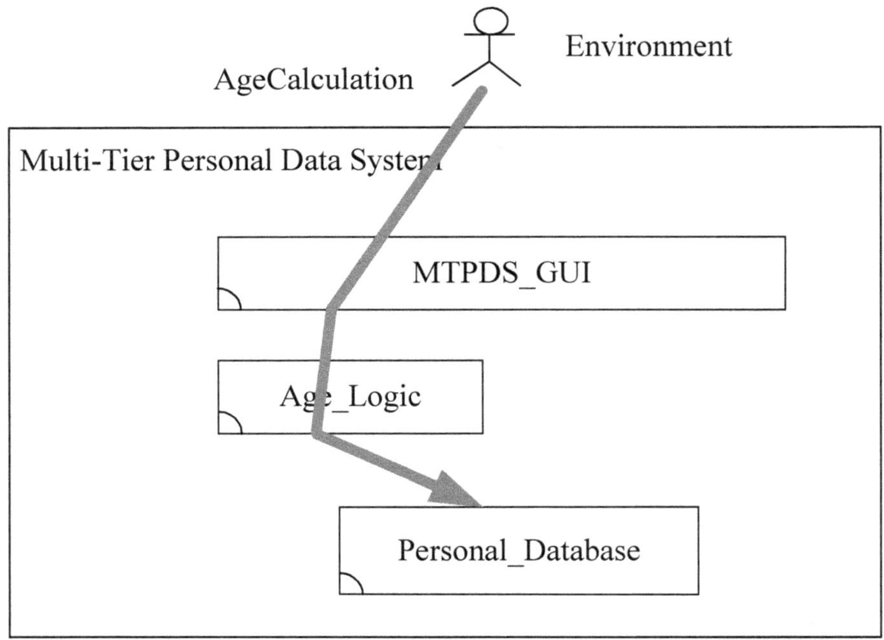

Figure 2-5 Interactions that Draw forth the *AgeCalculation* Behavior

As a second example, Figure 2-6 demonstrates that interactions between and among the environment and the *MTPDS_GUI*, *Overweight_Logic* and *Personal_Database* components shall draw forth the *OverweightCalculation* behavior.

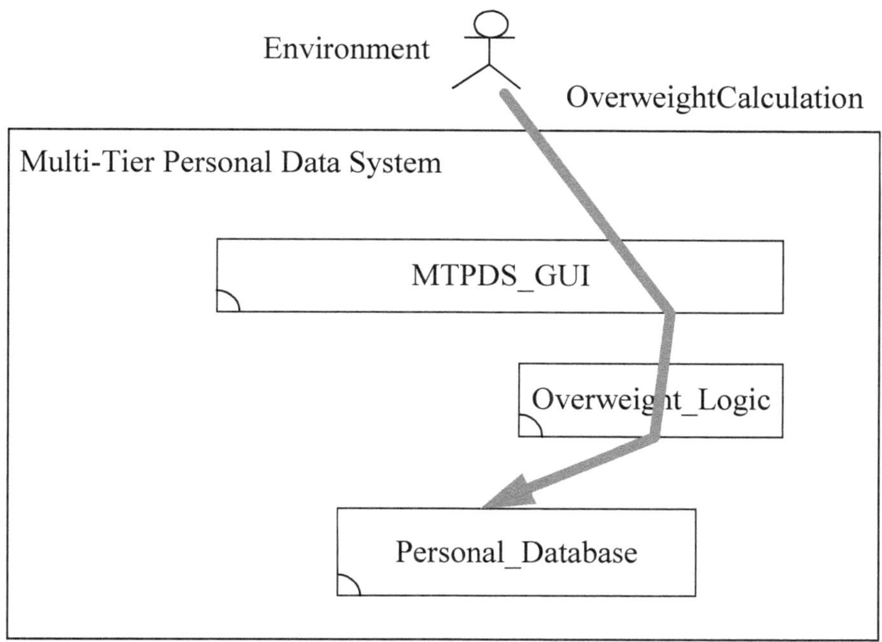

Figure 2-6 Interactions that Draw forth the *OverweightCalculation* Behavior

Chapter 3: Structure-Behavior Coalescence

A system has been described and represented hopefully to be an integrated whole, embodied in its assembled components, their interactions with each other and the environment. Since systems structure and systems behavior are the two most prominent views of a system, integrating the systems structure and systems behavior apparently is the best way to achieve a truly integrated whole of a system. Since knowledge representation 1.0 does not describe and represent the integration of systems structure and systems behavior, very likely it will never be able to actually form an integrated whole of a system.

Structure-behavior coalescence (SBC) provides an elegant way to integrate the systems structure and systems behavior, and hence achieves a truly integrated whole, of a system. A truly integrated whole sets a path to achieve the desired knowledge representation. SBC facilitates an integrated whole. Therefore, we conclude that SBC sets a path to achieve the knowledge representation. Knowledge representation 2.0 uses the SBC approach and is highly adequate in describing and representing a system.

3-1 Integrated Whole to Achieve the Knowledge Representation

A system has been described and represented hopefully to be an integrated whole, embodied in its assembled components, their interactions with each other and the environment. In other words, an integrated whole sets a path to achieve the knowledge representation as shown in Figure 3-1.

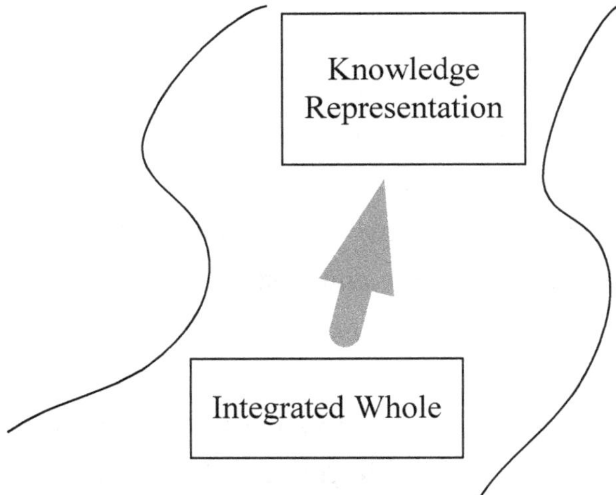

Figure 3-1 Integrated Whole to Achieve the Knowledge Representation

In one knowledge representation, different systems structures may draw forth the same integrated whole as shown in Figure 3-2.

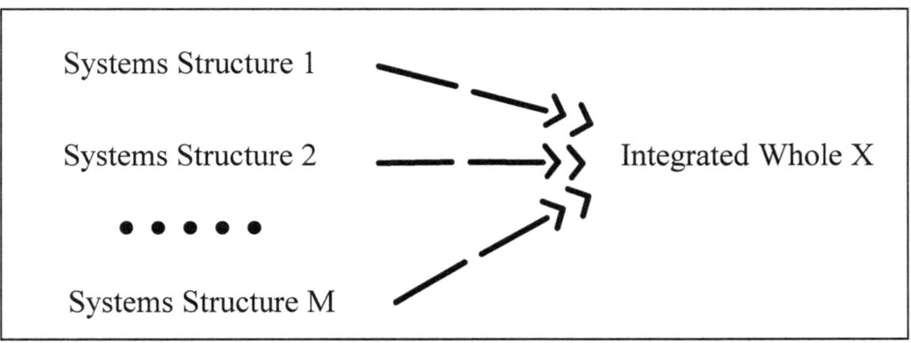

Figure 3-2 Different Systems Structures Draw Forth the Same Integrated Whole

Since there is only one systems structure exists in one knowledge representation, one systems structure will draw forth one integrated whole as shown in Figure 3-3.

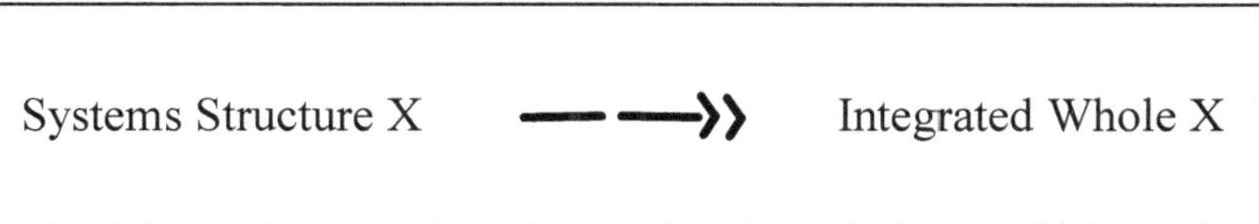

Figure 3-3 One Systems Structure Draws Forth One Integrated Whole

We conclude that in one knowledge representation, an integrated whole must be attached to or built on a systems structure. In other words, an integrated whole shall not exist alone; it must be loaded on a systems structure just like a cargo is loaded on a ship as shown in Figure 3-4. There will be no integrated whole if there is no systems structure. A stand-alone integrated whole with no systems structure is not meaningful.

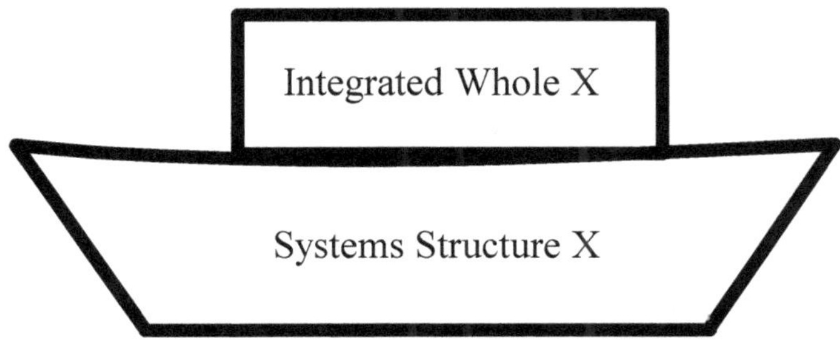

Figure 3-4 An Integrated Whole Must be Loaded on a Systems Structure

3-2 Integrating the Systems Structure and Systems Behavior

By integrating the systems structures and systems behaviors, we obtain structure-behavior coalescence (SBC) within a system. Since systems structures and systems behaviors are so tightly integrated, we sometimes claim that the core theme of structure-behavior coalescence is: "Systems Architecture = Systems Structure + Systems Behavior," as shown in Figure 3-5.

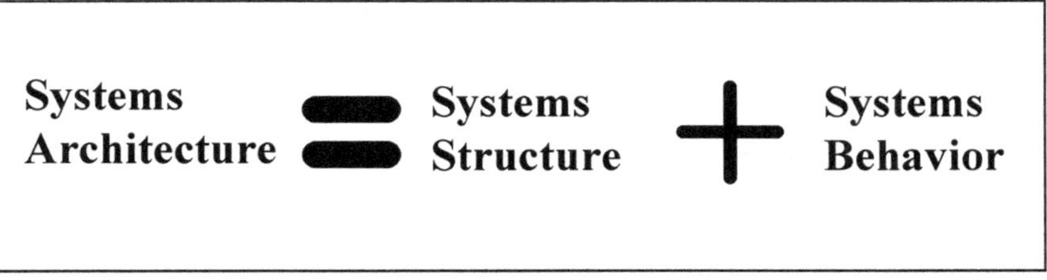

Figure 3-5 Core Theme of Structure-Behavior Coalescence

So far, integrating the systems structure and systems behavior has never been proposed or suggested besides the SBC approach. In most cases, systems behaviors are separated from systems structures when describing and representing a system [Hoff10, Pres09, Shel11, Somm06].

3-3 Structure-Behavior Coalescence to Facilitate an Integrated Whole

Since systems structure and systems behavior are the two most prominent views of a system, integrating the systems structure and systems behavior apparently is the best way to achieve a truly integrated whole of a system. If we are not able to integrate the systems structure and systems behavior, then there is no way that we are able to integrate the whole system. In other words, structure-behavior coalescence (SBC) facilitates a truly integrated whole as shown in Figure 3-6.

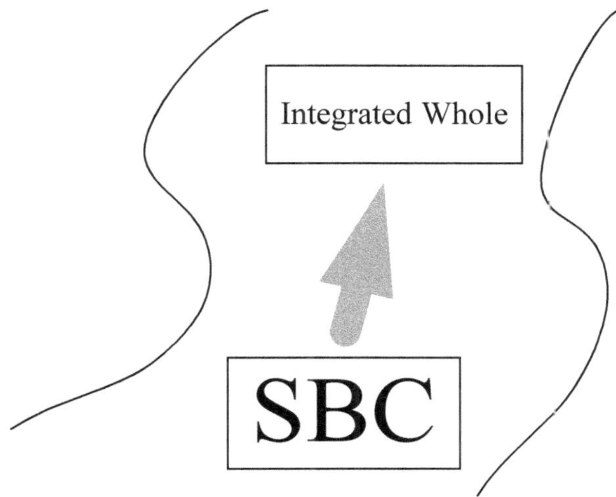

Figure 3-6 SBC Facilitates an Integrated Whole

Since knowledge representation 1.0 does not describe and represent the integration of systems structure and systems behavior, very likely it will never be able to actually form an integrated whole of a system. In this situation, knowledge representation 1.0 is powerless in describing and representing a system adequately.

3-4 Structure-Behavior Coalescence to Achieve the Knowledge Representation

Figure 3-1 declares that an integrated whole sets a path to achieve the desired knowledge representation. Figure 3-6 declares that structure-behavior coalescence facilitates a truly integrated whole.

Combining the above two declarations, we conclude that the structure-behavior coalescence (SBC) approach sets a path to achieve the knowledge representation as shown in Figure 3-7.

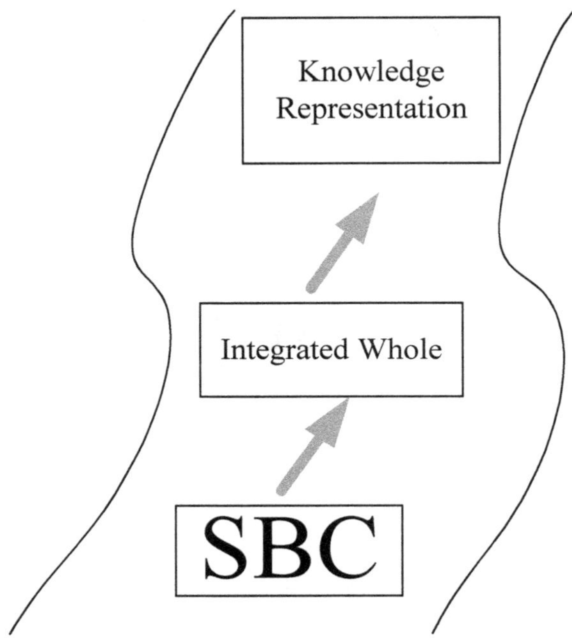

Figure 3-7 SBC to Achieve the Knowledge Representation

In the SBC approach, different systems structures may draw forth the same systems behavior as shown in Figure 3-8.

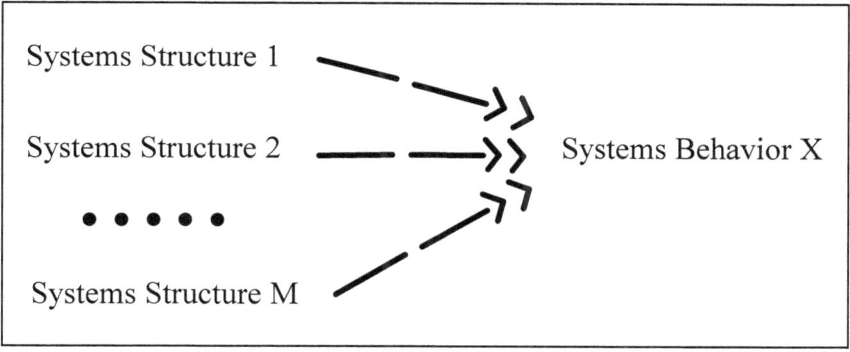

Figure 3-8 Different Systems Structures Draw Forth the Same Systems Behavior

Since there is only one systems structure exists in one knowledge representation, one systems behavior will always be attached to or built on one systems structure as shown in Figure 3-9.

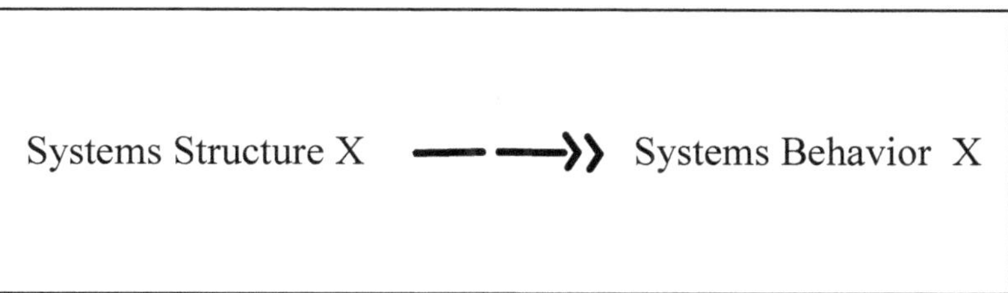

Figure 3-9 One Systems Behavior is Attached to One Systems Structure

We conclude that in the SBC approach, a systems behavior must be attached to or built on a systems structure. In other words, a systems behavior can not exist alone; it must be loaded on a systems structure just like a cargo is loaded on a ship as shown in Figure 3-10. There will be no systems behavior if there is no systems structure. A stand-alone systems behavior with no systems structure is not meaningful.

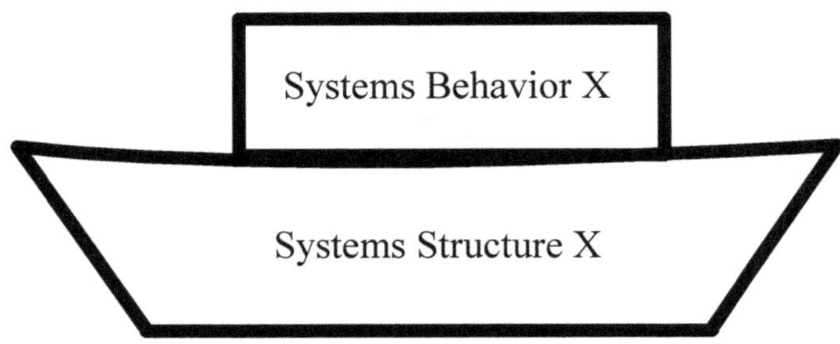

Figure 3-10 A Systems Behavior Must be Loaded on a Systems Structure

3-5 SBC Approach for Knowledge Representation 2.0

Since structure-behavior coalescence (SBC) provides an elegant way to integrate the systems structure and systems behavior, we shall include it in the knowledge representation of a system. Figure 3-11 shows how the knowledge representation 2.0 describes and represents a system.

A system,
through the SBC approach,
truly is an integrated whole,
embodied in its assembled components,
their interactions with each other and the environment.

Figure 3-11 Knowledge Representation 2.0
Describing and Representing a System

A system described and represented by the knowledge representation 2.0 has the following characteristics: 1) it emphasizes the system's structure-behavior coalescence; 2) it is a truly integrated whole; 3) it is embodied in its assembled components; 4) components are interacting (or handshaking) [Chao15a, Chao15b, Chao15c, Chao15d, Chao15e, Hoar85, Miln89, Miln99] with each other and the environment; and 5) it uses structural decomposition [Chao14a, Chao14b, Chao14c, Ghar11] rather than functional decomposition [Scho10].

Structure-behavior coalescence (SBC) provides an elegant way to integrate the systems structure and systems behavior of a system. Knowledge representation 2.0 uses the SBC approach to formally describe and represent the integration of systems structure and systems behavior of a system. Knowledge representation 2.0 contains three fundamental diagrams: a) framework diagram, b) component operation diagram and c) interaction flow diagram.

So far, we have introduced the knowledge representation 2.0 which should be able to appropriately describe and represent a system. In the following chapters, we shall elaborate the details of the knowledge representation 2.0..

3-6 SBC Model Singularity

Channel-Based Single-Queue SBC Process Algebra (C-S-SBC-PA) [Chao17a], Channel-Based Multi-Queue SBC Process Algebra (C-M-SBC-PA) [Chao17b], Channel-Based Infinite-Queue SBC Process Algebra (C-I-SBC-PA) [Chao17c], Operation-Based Single-Queue SBC Process Algebra (O-S-SBC-PA) [Chao17d], Operation-Based Multi-Queue SBC Process Algebra (O-M-SBC-PA) [Chao17e] and Operation-Based Infinite-Queue SBC Process Algebra (O-I-SBC-PA) [Chao17f] are the six specialized SBC process algebras. The SBC process algebra (SBC-PA) shown in Figure 3-12 is a model singularity approach.

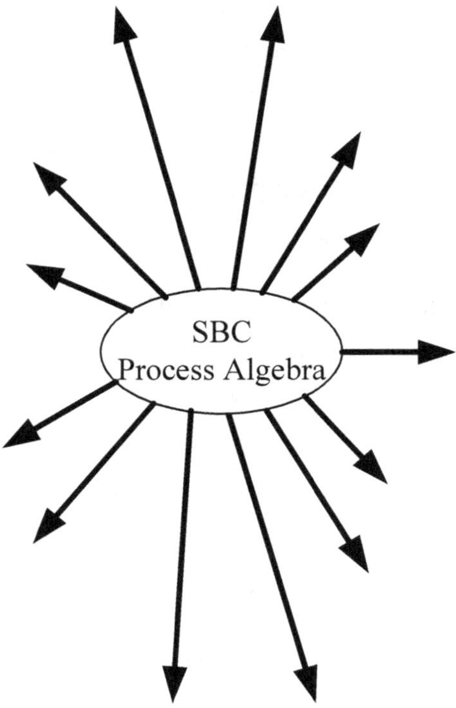

Figure 3-12 SBC-PA is a Model Singularity Approach.

The knowledge representation 2.0 is also a model singularity approach. With SBC mind set sitting in the kernel, the knowledge representation 2.0 single model shown in Figure 3-13 is therefore able to represent all structural views such as framework diagram (FD), component operation diagram (COD), and behavioral views such as interaction flow diagram (IFD).

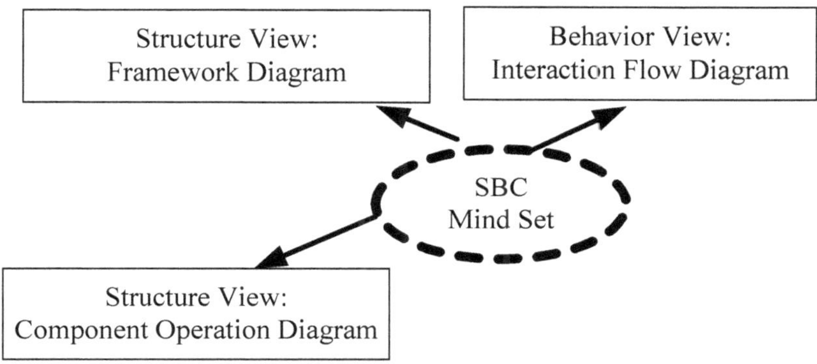

Figure 3-13 Knowledge Representation 2.0 is a Model Singularity Approach.

The combination of SBC process algebra (SBC-PA) and knowledge representation 2.0 is shown in Figure 3-14, again as a model singularity approach.

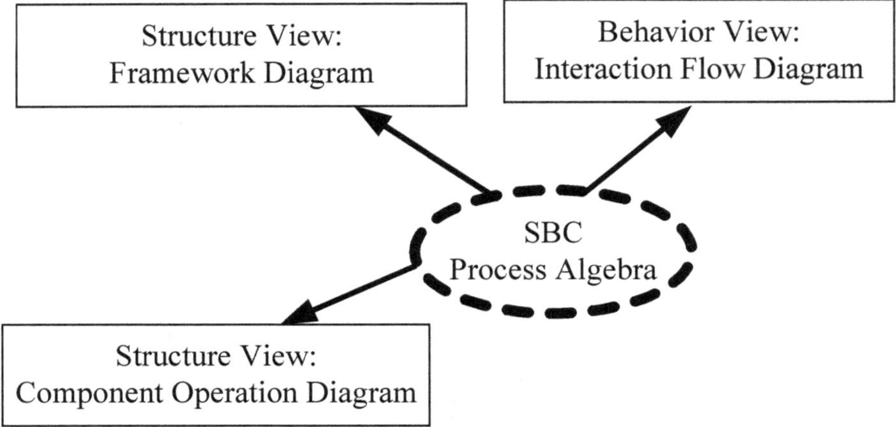

Figure 3-14 SBC Model is a Model Singularity Approach.

PART II: SBC APPROACH FOR KNOWLEDGE REPRESENTATION 2.0

Chapter 4: Framework Diagram

SBC approach for knowledge representation 2.0 uses a framework diagram (FD) to describe and represent the multi-layer (also referred to as multi-tier) decomposition and composition of a system.

4-1 Multi-Layer Decomposition and Composition

Decomposition and composition of a system can be described and represented in a multi-layer manner. We draw a framework diagram (FD) for the multi-layer decomposition and composition of a system.

As the first example, Figure 4-1 shows a FD of the *Multi-Tier Personal Data System*. In the figure, *Presentation_Layer* contains the *MTPDS_GUI* component; *Logic_Laye* contains the *Age_Logic* and *Overweight_Logic* components; *Data_Layer* contains the *Personal_Database* component.

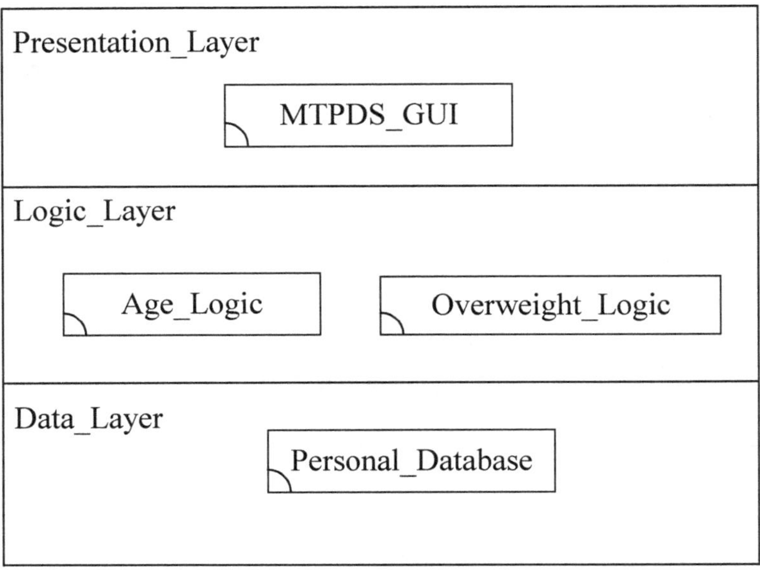

Figure 4-1 FD of the *Multi-Tier Personal Data System*

As the second example, Figure 4-2 shows a FD of the *human body*. In the figure, *Layer_3* contains the *Mouth*, *Nose* and *Hand* components; *Layer_2* contains the *Stomach*, *Intestine* and *Lung* components; *Layer_1* contains the *Blood_Vessel* and *Cells* components.

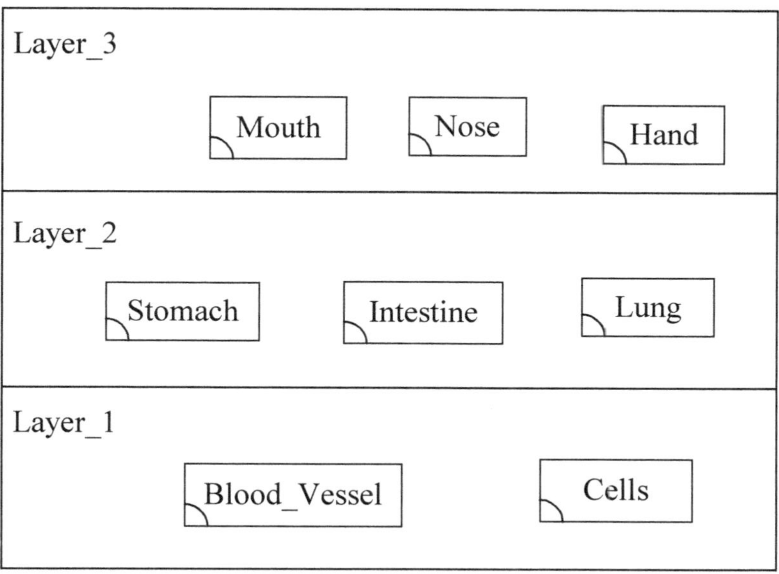

Figure 4-2 FD of the *Human Body*

4-2 Only Non-Aggregated Systems Appearing in Framework Diagrams

It is interesting that we see only non-aggregated systems shall appear in the multi-layer FD decomposition and composition of a system.

For the first example, Figure 4-1 in the previous section shows a FD of the *Multi-Tier Personal Data System* in which only non-aggregated systems such as *MTPDS_GUI*, *Age_Logic*, *Overweight_Logic* and *Personal_Database* are displayed.

For a second example, Figure 4-2 in the previous section shows a FD of the *human body* in which only non-aggregated systems such as *Mouth*, *Nose*, *Hand*, *Stomach*, *Intestine*, *Lung*, *Blood_Vessel*, *Cells* are displayed.

Chapter 5: Component Operation Diagram

SBC approach for knowledge representation 2.0 uses a component operation diagram (COD) to describe and represent all components' operations of a system.

5-1 Operations of Each Component

An operation provided by each component represents a procedure or method or function of the component. If other components request this component to perform an operation, then shall use it to accomplish the operation request.

Each component in a system must possess at least one operation. A component should not exist in a system if it does not possess any operation. Figure 5-1 shows that the *MTPDS_GUI* component has two operations: *Calculate_AgeClick* and *Calculate_OverweightClick.*

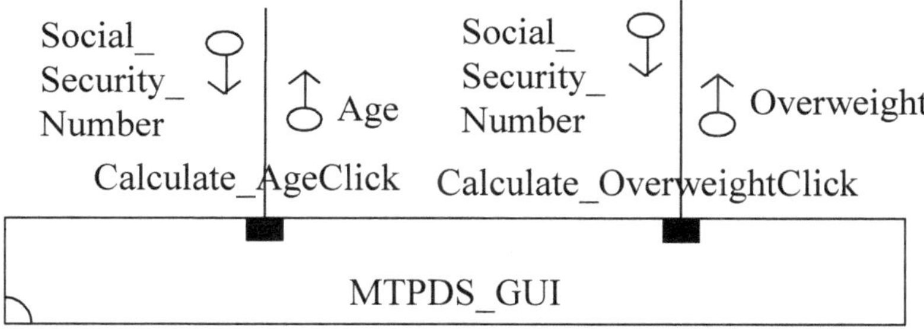

Figure 5-1 Two Operations of the *MTPDS_GUI* Component

An operation formula is utilized to fully represent an operation. An operation formula includes a) operation name, b) input parameters and c) output parameters as shown in Figure 5-2.

Operation_Name (In i_1, i_2, ..., i_m ; Out o_1 , o_2, ..., o_n)

Figure 5-2 Operation Formula

Operation name is the name of this operation. In a system, every operation name should be unique. Duplicate operation names shall not be allowed in any system.

An operation may have several input and output parameters. The input and output parameters, gathered from all operations, represent the input data and output data views of a system [Date03, Elma10]. As shown in Figure 5-3, component *Personal_Database* possesses the *Sql_DateOfBirth_Select* operation which has the *Social_Security_Number* input parameter (with the arrow direction pointing to the component) and the *query_DateOfBirth* output parameter (with the arrow direction opposite to the component); component *Personal_Database* also possesses the *Sql_SexHeightWeight_Select* operation which has the *Social_Security_Number* input parameter (with the arrow direction pointing to the component) and the *query_SexHeightWeight* output parameter (with the arrow direction opposite to the component).

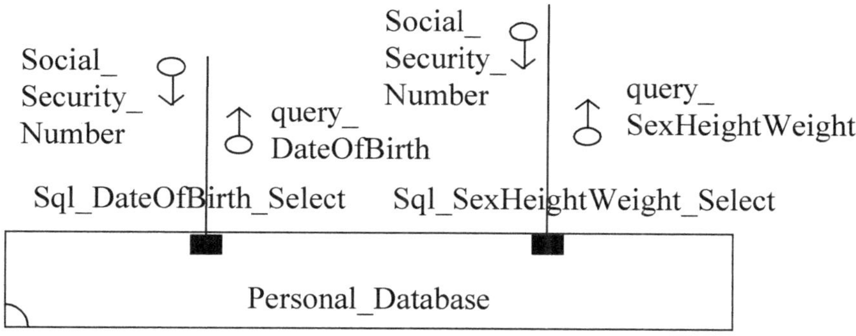

Figure 5-3 Input/Output Parameters

Data formats of input and output parameters can be described by data type specifications. There are two sets of data types: primitive and composite [Date03, Elma10]. Figure 5-4 shows the primitive data type specification of the *Social_Security_Number* input parameter occurring in the *Sql_DateOfBirth_Select(In Social_Security_Number; Out query_DateOfBirth)* operation formula.

Parameter	Data Type	Instances
Social_Security_Number	Text	424-87-3651

Figure 5-4 Primitive Data Type Specification

Figure 5-5 shows the composite data type specification of the *query_DateOfBirth* output parameter occurring in the *Sql_DateOfBirth_Select(In Social_Security_Number; Out query_DateOfBirth)* operation formula.

Parameter	*query_DateOfBirth*
Data Type	TABLE of Social_Security_Number : Text Age : Integer End TABLE;
Instances	424-87-3651 | 28 512-24-3722 | 56

Figure 5-5 Composite Data Type Specification of *query_DateOfBirth*

Figure 5-6 shows the composite data type specification of the *query_SexHeightWeight* output parameter occurring in the *Sql_SexHeightWeight_Select(In Social_Security_Number; Out query_SexHeightWeight)* operation formula.

<table>
<tr><td>Parameter</td><td>query_SexHeightWeight</td></tr>
<tr><td>Data Type</td><td>TABLE of
Social_Security_Number : Text
Sex : Text
Height : Number
Weight : Number
End TABLE;</td></tr>
<tr><td>Instances</td><td>424-87-3651 | Female | 162 | 76
512-24-3722 | Male | 180 | 80</td></tr>
</table>

Figure 5-6 Composite Data Type Specification of *query_SexHeightWeight*

5-2 Drawing the Component Operation Diagram

For a system, COD is used to describe and represent all components' operations. Figure 5-7 shows the *Multi-Tier Personal Data System's COD*. In the figure, component *MTPDS_GUI* has two operations: *Calculate_AgeClick* and *Calculate_OverweightClick*; component *Age_Logic* has one operation: *Calculate_Age*; component *Overweight_Logic* has one operation: *Calculate_Overweight*; component *Personal_Database* has two operations: *Sql_DateOfBirth_Select* and *Sql_SexHeightWeight_Select*.

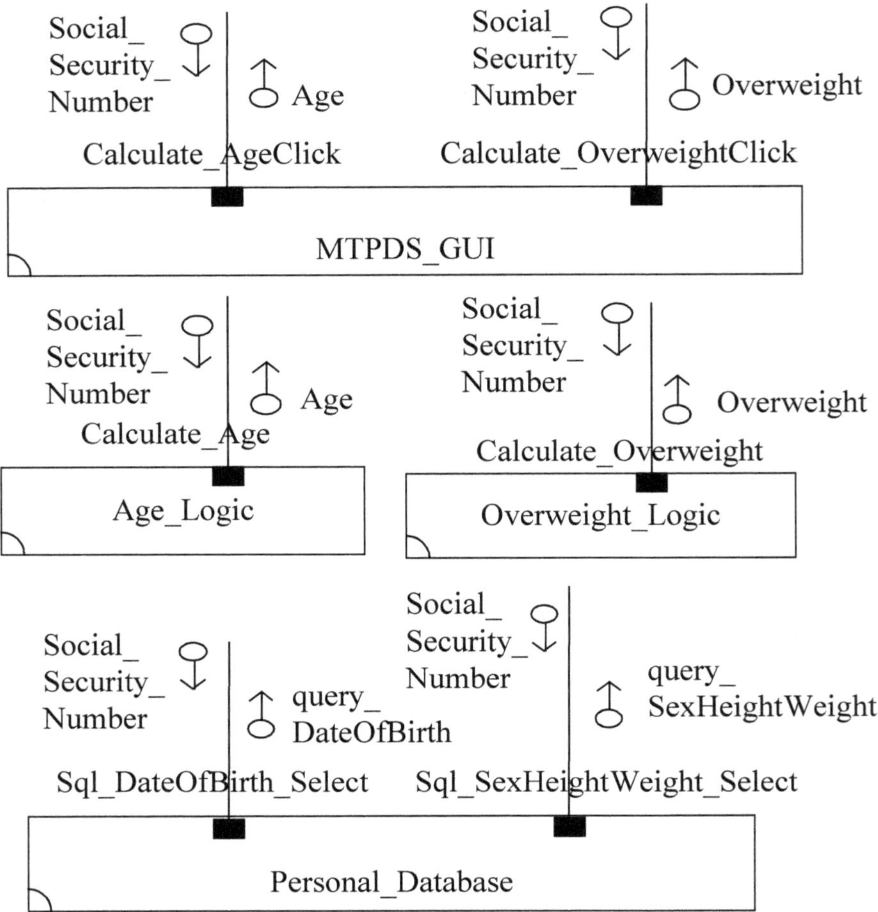

Figure 5-7 COD of the *Multi-Tier Personal Data System*

Chapter 6: Interaction Flow Diagram

SBC approach for knowledge representation 2.0 uses an interaction flow diagram (IFD) to describe and represent each individual behavior of the overall behavior of a system.

6-1 Individual Behavior Represented by Interaction Flow Diagram

The overall behavior of a system consists of many individual behaviors. Each individual behavior represents an execution path. An IFD is utilized to describe and represent such an individual behavior.

Figure 6-1 demonstrates that the *Multi-Tier Personal Data System* has two behaviors; thus, it has two IFDs.

System	IFD
Multi-Tier Personal Data System	AgeCalculation
	OverweightCalculation

Figure 6-1 *Multi-Tier Personal Data System* has Two IFDs

Figure 6-2 demonstrates that the *human body* has three behaviors; thus, it has three IFDs.

System	IFD
Human Body	Eating
	Respiring
	Combating

Figure 6-2 *Human Body* has Three IFDs

6-2 Drawing the Interaction Flow Diagram

Let us now explain the usage of interaction flow diagram (IFD) by drawing an IFD step by step. Figure 6-3 demonstrates an IFD of the *AgeCalculation* behavior. The X-axis direction is from the left side to right side and the Y-axis direction is from the above to the below. Inside an IFD, there are four elements: a) external environment's actor, b) components, c) interactions and d) input/output parameters. Participants of the interaction, such as the external environment's actor and each component, are laid aside along the X-axis direction on the top of the diagram. The external environment's actor which initiates the sequential interactions is always placed on the most left side of the X-axis. Then, interactions among the external environment's actor and components successively in turn decorate along the Y-axis direction. The first interaction is placed on the top of the Y-axis position. The last interaction is placed on the bottom of the Y-axis position. Each interaction may carry several input and/or output parameters.

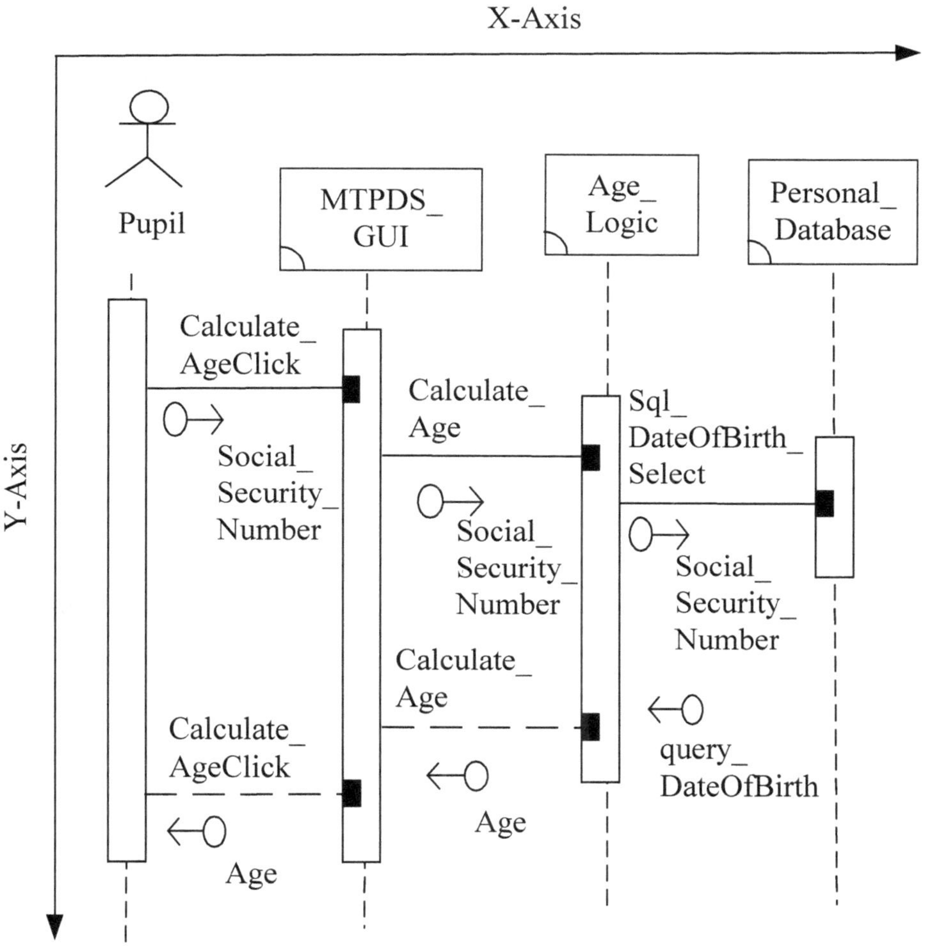

Figure 6-3 IFD of the *AgeCalculation* Behavior

In Figure 6-3, *Pupil* is an external environment's actor. *MTPDS_GUI*, *Age_Logic* and *Personal_Database* are components. *Calculate_AgeClick* is an operation, carrying the *Social_Security_Number* input parameter and *Age* output parameter, which is provided by the *MTPDS_GUI* component. *Calculate_Age* is an operation, carrying the *Social_Security_Number* input parameter and *Age* output parameter, which is provided by the *Age_Logic* component, *Sql_DateOfBirth_Select* is an operation, carrying the *Social_Security_Number* input parameter and *query_DateOfBirth* output parameter, which is provided by the *Personal_Database* component.

The execution path of Figure 6-3 is as follows. First, actor *Pupil* interacts with the *MTPDS_GUI* component through the *Calculate_AgeClick* operation call interaction, carrying the *Social_Security_Number* input parameter. Next, component *MTPDS_GUI* interacts with the *AgeCalculation* component through the *Calculate_Age* operation call interaction, carrying the *Social_Security_Number* input parameter. Continuingly, component *Age_Logic* interacts with the *Personal_Database* component through the *Sql_DateOfBirth_Select* operation call interaction, carrying the *Social_Security_Number* input parameter and the *query_DateOfBirth* output parameter. Repeatedly, component *MTPDS_GUI* interacts with the *Age_Logic* component through the *Calculate_Age* operation return interaction, carrying the *Age* output parameter. Finally, actor *Pupil* interacts with the *MTPDS_GUI* component through the *Calculate_AgeClick* operation return interaction, carrying the *Age* output parameter.

For each interaction, the solid line stands for operation call while the dashed line stands for operation return. The operation call and operation return interactions, if using the same operation name, belong to the identical operation. Figure 6-4 exhibits two interactions (operation call interaction and operation return interaction) having the identical "*Calculate_OverweightClick*" operation.

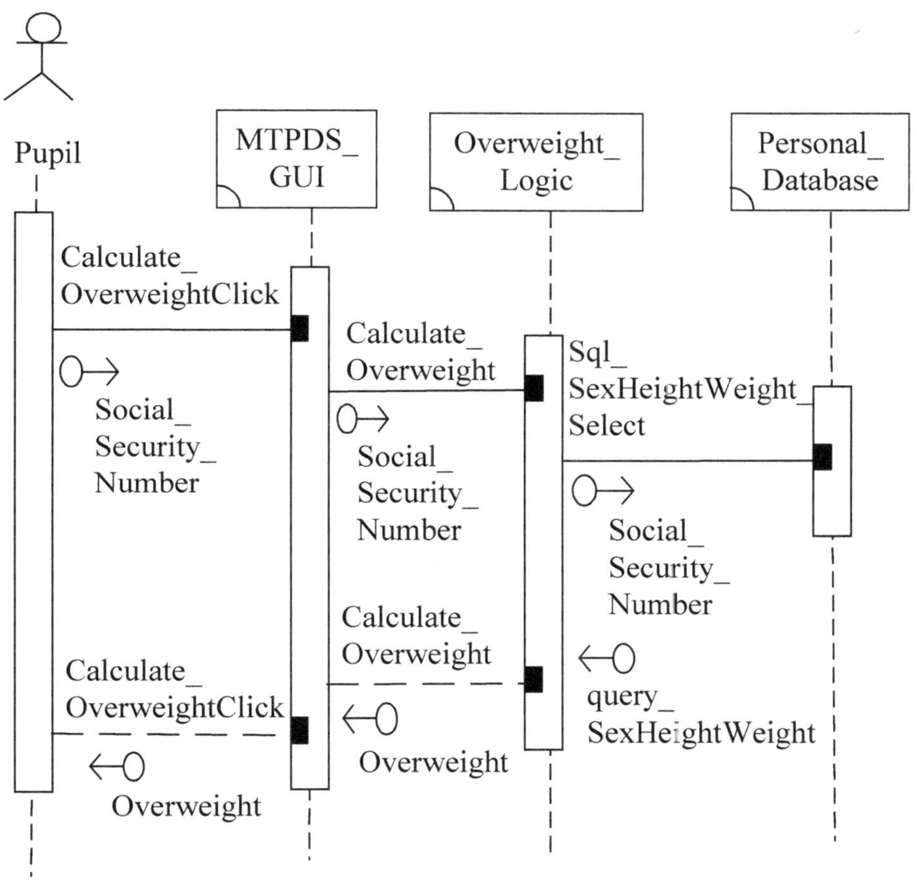

Figure 6-4 Two Interactions Have the Identical Operation

The execution path of Figure 6-4 is as follows. First, actor *Pupil* interacts with the *MTPDS_GUI* component through the *Calculate_OverweightClick* operation call interaction, carrying the *Social_Security_Number* input parameter. Next, component *MTPDS_GUI* interacts with the *OverweightCalculation* component through the *Calculate_Overweight* operation call interaction, carrying the

Social_Security_Number input parameter. Continuingly, component *Overweight_Logic* interacts with the *Personal_Database* component through the *Sql_SexHeightWeight_Select* operation call interaction, carrying the *Social_Security_Number* input parameter and the *query_SexHeightWeight* output parameter. Repeatedly, component *MTPDS_GUI* interacts with the *Overweight_Logic* component through the *Calculate_Overweight* operation return interaction, carrying the *Overweight* output parameter. Finally, actor *Pupil* interacts with the *MTPDS_GUI* component through the *Calculate_OverweightClick* operation return interaction, carrying the *Overweight* output parameter.

An interaction flow diagram may contain a conditional expression. Figure 6-5 shows such an example which has the following execution path. First, external environment's actor *Employee* interacts with the *Computer* component through the *Open* operation call interaction, carrying the *Task_No* input parameter. Next, if the *var_1 < 4 & var_2 > 7* condition is true then component *Computer* shall interact with the *Skype* component through the *Op_1* operation call interaction and component *Skype* shall interact with the *Earphone* component through the *Op_4* operation call interaction, carrying the *Skype_Earphone* output parameter; else if the *var_3 = 99* condition is true then component *Computer* shall interact with the *Skype* component through the *Op_2* operation call interaction and component *Skype* shall interact with the *Speaker* component through the *Op_5* operation call interaction, carrying the *Skype_Speaker* output parameter; else component *Computer* shall interact with the *Youtube* component through the *Op_3* operation call interaction and component *Youtube* shall interact with the *Speaker* component through the *Op_6* operation call interaction, carrying the *Youtube_Speaker* output parameter. Continuingly, if the *var_1 < 4 & var_2 > 7* condition is true then component *Computer* shall interact with the *Skype* component through the *Op_1* operation return interaction, carrying the *Status_1* output parameter; else if the *var_3* = *99* condition is true then component *Computer* shall interact with the *Skype* component through the *Op_2* operation return interaction, carrying the *Status_2* output parameter; else component *Computer* shall interact with the *Youtube* component through the *Op_3* operation return interaction, carrying the *Status_3* output parameter. Finally, external environment's actor *Employee* interacts with the *Computer* component through the *Open* operation return interaction, carrying the *Status* output parameter.

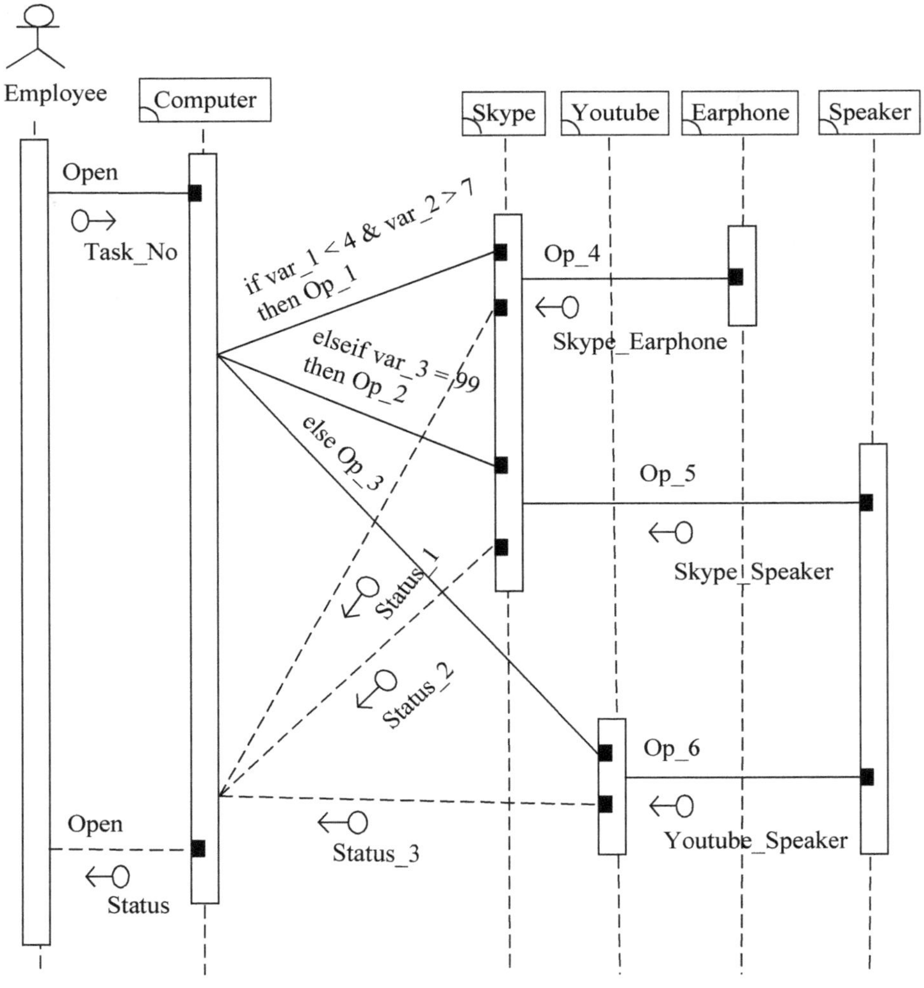

Figure 6-5 Conditional Interaction

Several Boolean conditions are shown in Figure 6-5. They are "*var_1 < 4 & var_2 > 7*" and "*var_3 = 99*". Variables, such as *var_1*, *var_2* and *var_3*, appearing in the Boolean condition can be local or global variables [Prat00, Seth96].

PART III: CASES STUDY

Chapter 7: Knowledge Representation 2.0 of the Multi-Tier Personal Data System

This chapter examines the *Multi-Tier Personal Data System* which represents a case study of knowledge representation 2.0, using the structure-behavior coalescence approach. After the systems development is finished, the *Multi-Tier Personal Data System* shall appear on a multi-tier platform [Wall04] as shown in Figure 7-1.

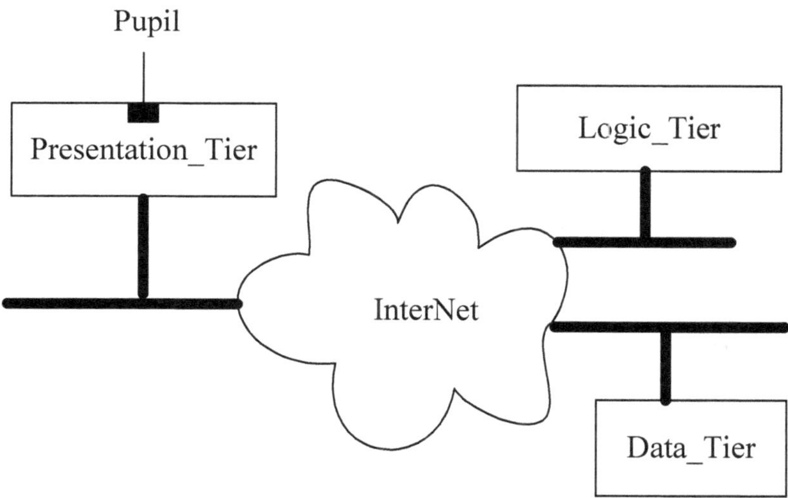

Figure 7-1 *Multi-Tier Personal Data System* on a Multi-Tier Platform

In the *Data_Tier*, there is a *Personal_Database* database [Date03, Elma10] which contains a *Personal_Data* table as shown in Figure 7-2.

Personal_Database : Database

Personal_Data : Table

Social_Security_Number	Name	Date_of_Birth	Sex	Height (cm)	Weight (Kg)
318-49-2465	Mary R. Williams	June 17, 1976	Female	165	51
424-87-3651	Lee H. Wulf	July 24, 1982	Female	162	76
512-24-3722	John K. Bryant	May 12, 1954	Male	180	80

Figure 7-2 *Personal_Database* Contains *Personal_Data*

The overall behavior of the *Multi-Tier Personal Data System* is to provide a graphical user interface (GUI) [Gali07] for the *Pupil* actor to trigger two behaviors. The first behavior is *AgeCalculation* and the second behavior is *OverweightCalculation*, as shown in Figure 7-3.

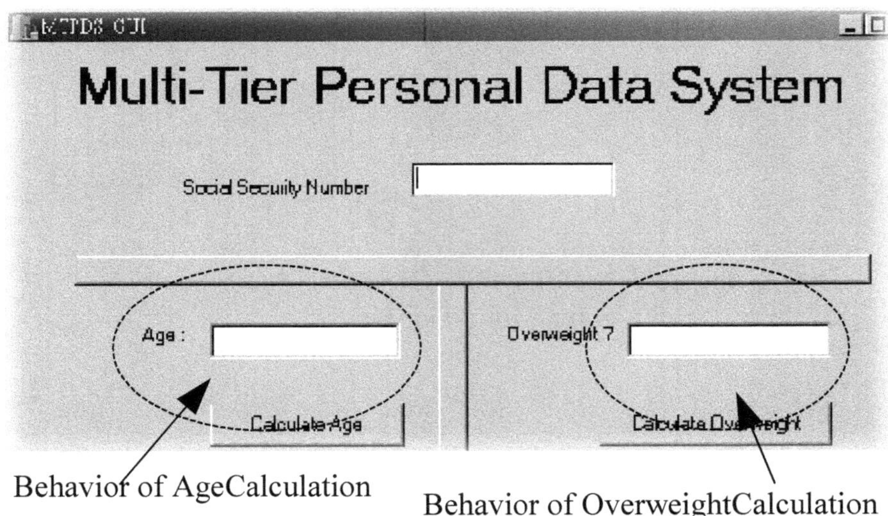

Figure 7-3 Two Behaviors

In the *AgeCalculation* behavior, actor *Pupil* inputs an integer *Social_Security_Number* value then presses down the *Calculate_Age* button. After that, the *Multi-Tier Personal Data System* retrieves the *Date_of_Birth* value from the database in line with the corresponding *Social_Security_Number* value. From the *Date_of_Birth* value, the *Multi-Tier Personal Data System* calculates the *Age* value and displays it on the screen. Figure 7-4 shows the *Social_Security_Number* value is 512-24-3722 and the retrieved *Date_of_Birth* value is May 12, 1954 and the calculated *Age* value, which is 61, is then displayed on the screen.

Personal_Data : Table

Social_Secuirty_Number	Date_of_Birth
318-49-2465	June 17, 1976
424-87-3651	July 24, 1982
512-24-3722	May 12, 1954

the calculated *Age* value when *Date_of_Birth* is May 12, 1954

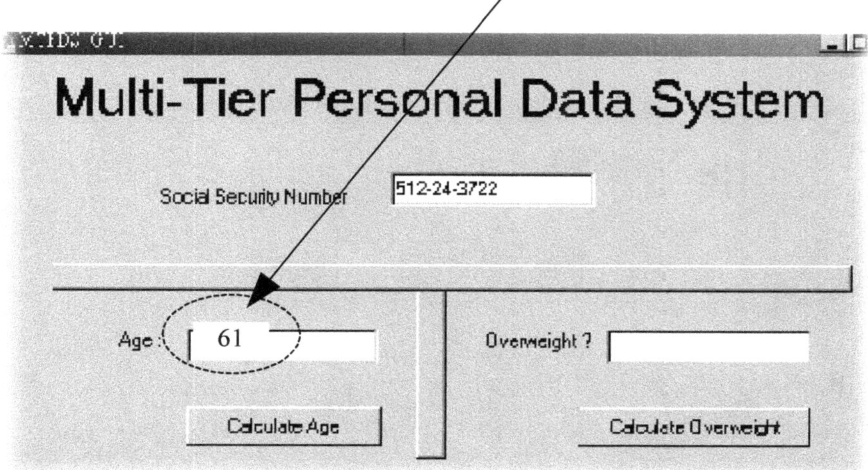

Figure 7-4 Behavior of *AgeCalculation*

In the *OverweightCalculation* behavior, actor *Pupil* inputs an integer *Social_Security_Number* value then presses down the *Calculate_Overweight* button. After that, the *Multi-Tier Personal Data System* retrieves the *Sex*, *Height* and *Weight* values from the database in line with the corresponding *Social_Security_Number* value. From the *Sex*, *Height* and *Weight* values, the *Multi-Tier Personal Data System* calculates the true-or-false Overweight value and displays it on the screen. Figure 7-5 shows the *Social_Security_Number* value is 318-49-2465 and the retrieved *Sex*, *Height* and *Weight* values are Female, 165 and 51, respectively, the calculated Overweight value, which is *No*, is then displayed on the screen.

Personal_Data : Table

Social_Secuirty_Number	Sex	Height (cm)	Weight (Kg)
318-49-2465	Female	165	51
424-87-3651	Female	162	76
512-24-3722	Male	180	80

the calculated *Overweight* value when Sex, Height (cm), and Weight (Kg) are Female, 165, and 51

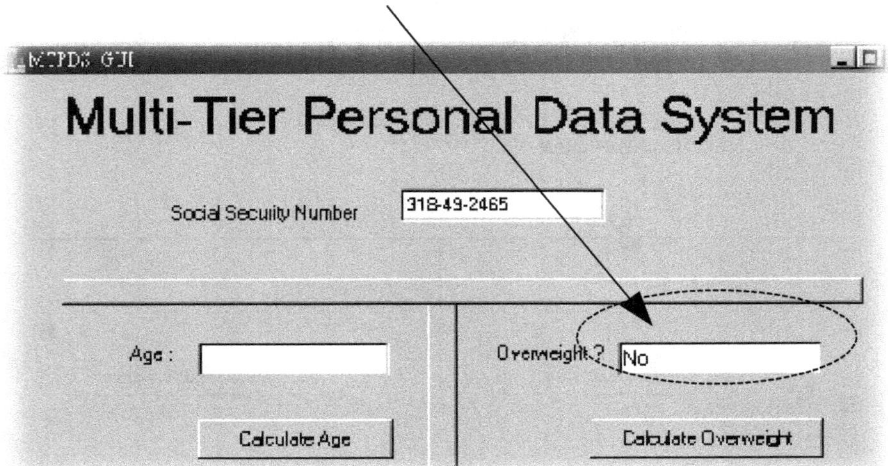

Figure 7-5 Behavior of *OverweightCalculation*

Using the structure-behavior coalescence (SBC) approach, we shall go through: a) framework diagram, b) component operation diagram and c) interaction flow diagram, to accomplish the knowledge representation 2.0 of the *Multi-Tier Personal Data System*.

7-1 Framework Diagram

Knowledge representation 2.0 uses a framework diagram (FD) to describe and represent the multi-layer composition and decomposition of the *Multi-Tier Personal Data System* as shown in Figure 7-6. In the figure, *Presentation_Layer* contains the *MTPDS_GUI* component; *Logic_Layer* contains the *Age_Logic* and *Overweight_Logic* components; *Data_Layer* contains the *Personal_Database* component.

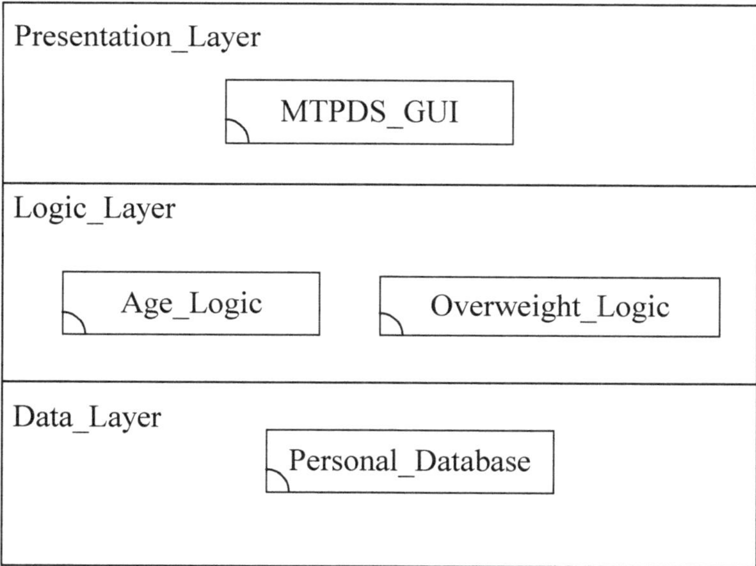

Figure 7-6 FD of the *Multi-Tier Personal Data System*

7-2 Component Operation Diagram

Knowledge representation 2.0 uses a component operation diagram (COD) to describe and represent the operations of all components of the *Multi-Tier Personal Data System* as shown in Figure 7-7. In the figure, component *MTPDS_GUI* has two operations: *Calculate_AgeClick* and *Calculate_OverweightClick*; component *Age_Logic* has one operation: *Calculate_Age*; component *Overweight_Logic* has one operation: *Calculate_Overweight*; component *Personal_Database* has two operations: *Sql_DateOfBirth_Select* and *Sql_SexHeightWeight_Select*.

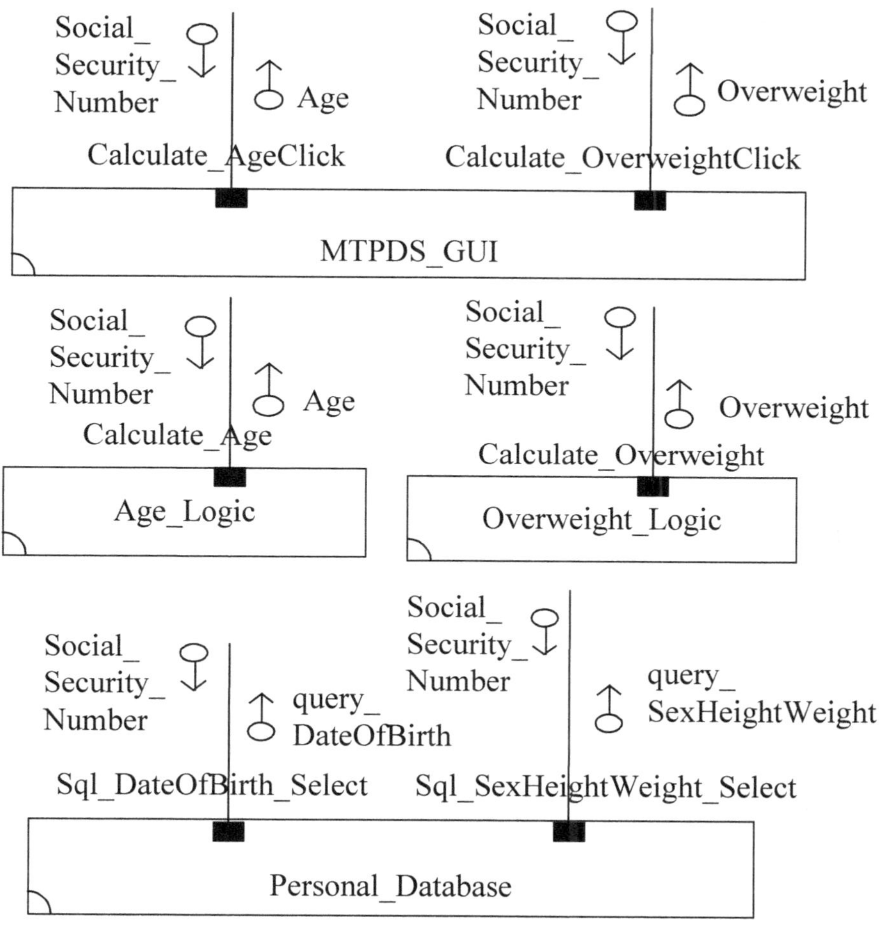

Figure 7-7 COD of the *Multi-Tier Personal Data System*

The operation formula of *Calculate_AgeClick* is *Calculate_AgeClick(In Social_Security_Number; Out Age)*. The operation formula of *Calculate_OverweightClick* is *Calculate_OverweightClick(In Social_Security_Number; Out Overweight)*. The operation formula of *Calculate_Age* is *Calculate_Age(In Social_Security_Number; Out Age)*. The operation formula of *Calculate_Overweight* is *Calculate_Overweight(In Social_Security_Number; Out Overweight)*. The operation formula of *Sql_DateOfBirth_Select* is *Sql_DateOfBirth_Select(In Social_Security_Number; Out query_DateOfBirth)*. The operation formula of *Sql_SexHeightWeight_Select* is *Sql_SexHeightWeight_Select(In Social_Security_Number; Out query_SexHeightWeight)*.

Figure 7-8 shows the primitive data type specification of the *Social_Security_Number* input parameter and the *Age*, *Overweight* output parameters.

Parameter	Data Type	Instances
Social_Security_Number	Text	424-87-3651
Age	Integer	28, 56
Overweight	Boolean	Yes, No

Figure 7-8 Primitive Data Type Specification

Figure 7-9 shows the composite data type specification of the *query_DateOfBirth* output parameter occurring in the *Sql_DateOfBirth_Select(In Social_Security_Number; Out query_DateOfBirth)* operation formula.

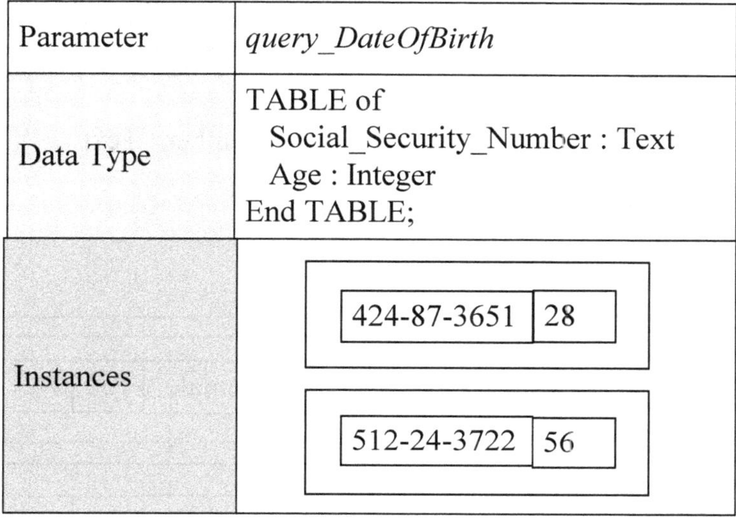

Parameter	*query_DateOfBirth*
Data Type	TABLE of Social_Security_Number : Text Age : Integer End TABLE;
Instances	424-87-3651 | 28 512-24-3722 | 56

Figure 7-9 Composite Data Type Specification

Figure 7-10 shows the composite data type specification of the *query_SexHeightWeight* output parameter occurring in the *Sql_SexHeightWeight_Select(In Social_Security_Number; Out query_SexHeightWeight)* operation formula.

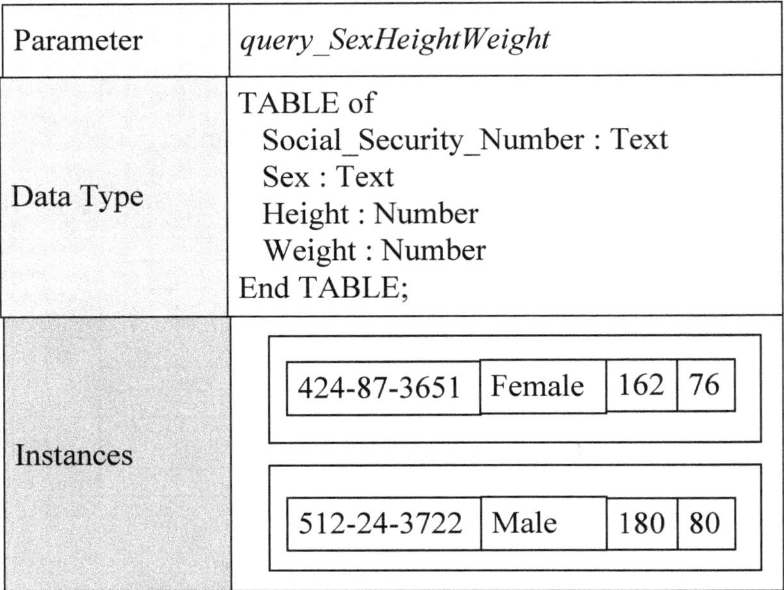

Parameter	*query_SexHeightWeight*
Data Type	TABLE of Social_Security_Number : Text Sex : Text Height : Number Weight : Number End TABLE;
Instances	424-87-3651 | Female | 162 | 76 512-24-3722 | Male | 180 | 80

Figure 7-10 Composite Data Type Specification

7-3 Interaction Flow Diagram

The overall behavior of the *Multi-Tier Personal Data System* includes two individual behaviors: *AgeCalculation* and *OverweightCalculation*. Each individual behavior is described and represented by an execution path. Knowledge representation 2.0 uses an IFD to describe and represent each one of these execution paths.

Figure 7-11 shows an IFD of the *AgeCalculation* behavior. First, actor *Pupil* interacts with the *MTPDS_GUI* component through the *Calculate_AgeClick* operation call interaction, carrying the *Social_Security_Number* input parameter. Next, component *MTPDS_GUI* interacts with the *AgeCalculation* component through the

Calculate_Age operation call interaction, carrying the *Social_Security_Number* input parameter. Continuingly, component *Age_Logic* interacts with the *Personal_Database* component through the *Sql_DateOfBirth_Select* operation call interaction, carrying the *Social_Security_Number* input parameter and the *query_DateOfBirth* output parameter. Repeatedly, component *MTPDS_GUI* interacts with the *Age_Logic* component through the *Calculate_Age* operation return interaction, carrying the *Age* output parameter. Finally, actor *Pupil* interacts with the *MTPDS_GUI* component through the *Calculate_AgeClick* operation return interaction, carrying the *Age* output parameter.

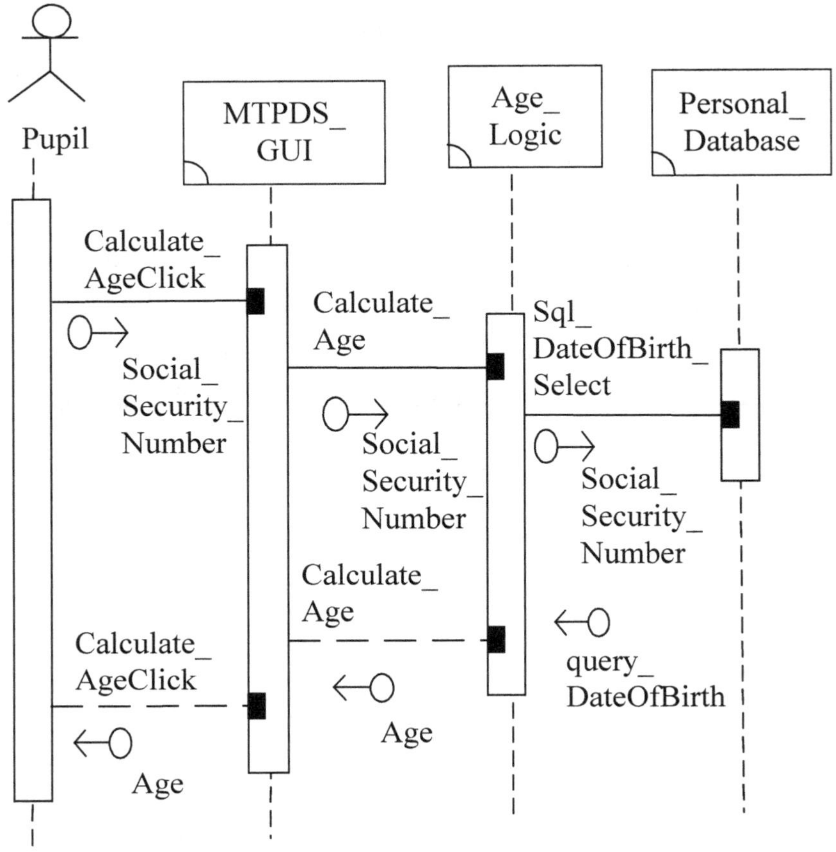

Figure 7-11 IFD of the *AgeCalculation* Behavior

Figure 7-12 shows an IFD of the *OverweightCalculation* behavior. First, actor *Pupil* interacts with the *MTPDS_GUI* component through the *Calculate_OverweightClick* operation call interaction, carrying the *Social_Security_Number* input parameter. Next, component *MTPDS_GUI* interacts with the *OverweightCalculation* component through the *Calculate_Overweight* operation call interaction, carrying the *Social_Security_Number* input parameter. Continuingly, component

Overweight_Logic interacts with the *Personal_Database* component through the *Sql_SexHeightWeight_Select* operation call interaction, carrying the *Social_Security_Number* input parameter and the *query_SexHeightWeight* output parameter. Repeatedly, component *MTPDS_GUI* interacts with the *Overweight_Logic* component through the *Calculate_Overweight* operation return interaction, carrying the *Overweight* output parameter. Finally, actor *Pupil* interacts with the *MTPDS_GUI* component through the *Calculate_OverweightClick* operation return interaction, carrying the *Overweight* output parameter.

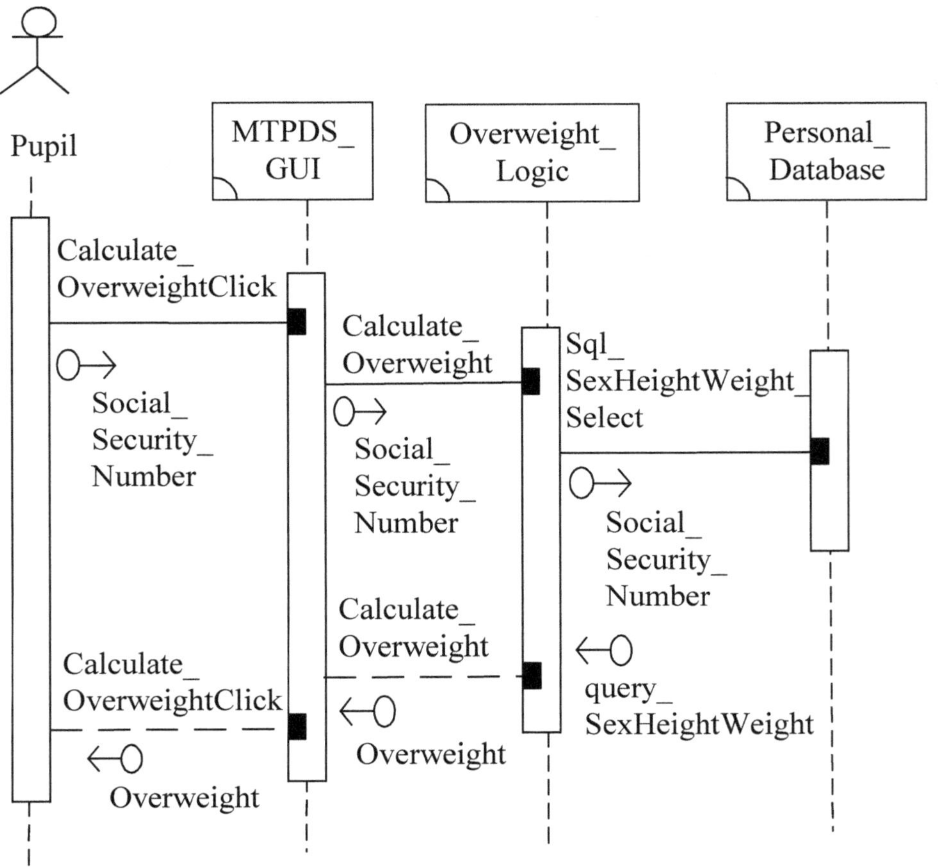

Figure 7-12 IFD of the *OverweightCalculation* Behavior

Chapter 8: Knowledge Representation 2.0 of the Human Body

In general, the overall behavior of the *human body* is prominently represented by three individual behaviors: *Eating*, *Respiring* and *Combating* as shown in Figure 8-1.

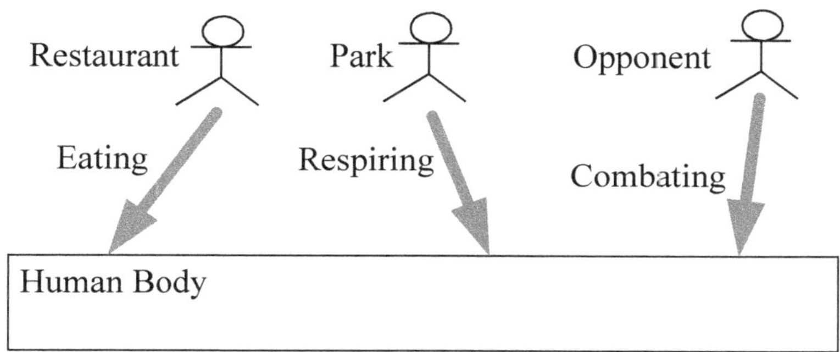

Figure 8-1 Three Behaviors of the *Human Body*

Using the structure-behavior coalescence (SBC) approach, we shall go through: a) framework diagram, b) component operation diagram and c) interaction flow diagram, to accomplish the knowledge representation 2.0 of the *human body*.

7-1 Framework Diagram

Knowledge representation 2.0 uses a framework diagram (FD) to describe and represent the multi-layer composition and decomposition of the *human body* as shown in Figure 8-2.

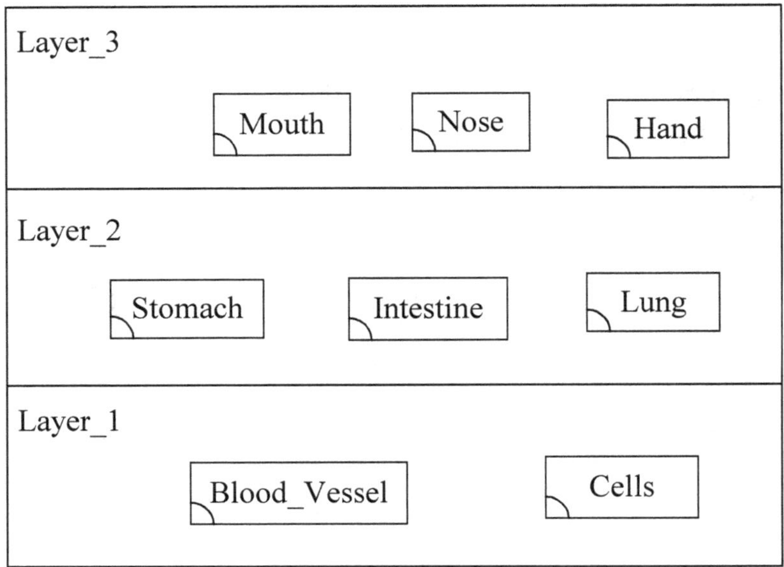

Figure 8-2 FD of the *Human Body*

In the above figure, *Layer_3* contains the *Mouth*, *Nose* and *Hand* components; *Layer_2* contains the *Stomach*, *Intestine* and *Lung* components; *Layer_1* contains the *Blood_Vessel* and *Cells* components.

7-2 Component Operation Diagram

Knowledge representation 2.0 uses a component operation diagram (COD) to describe and represent the operations of all components of the *human body* as shown in Figure 8-3. In the figure, component *Mouth* has one operation: *Chew*; component *Nose* has one operation: *Breathe*; component *Stomach* has one operation: *Digest*; component *Lung* has one operation: *Exchange_gas*; component *Hand* has one operation: *Punch*;

component *Intestine* has one operation: *Absorb_nutrients*; component *Blood_Vessel* has two operations: *Transport_nutrients* and *Transport_gas*; component *Eggs* has three operations: *Store_nutrients*, *Respire* and *Consume_nutrients*.

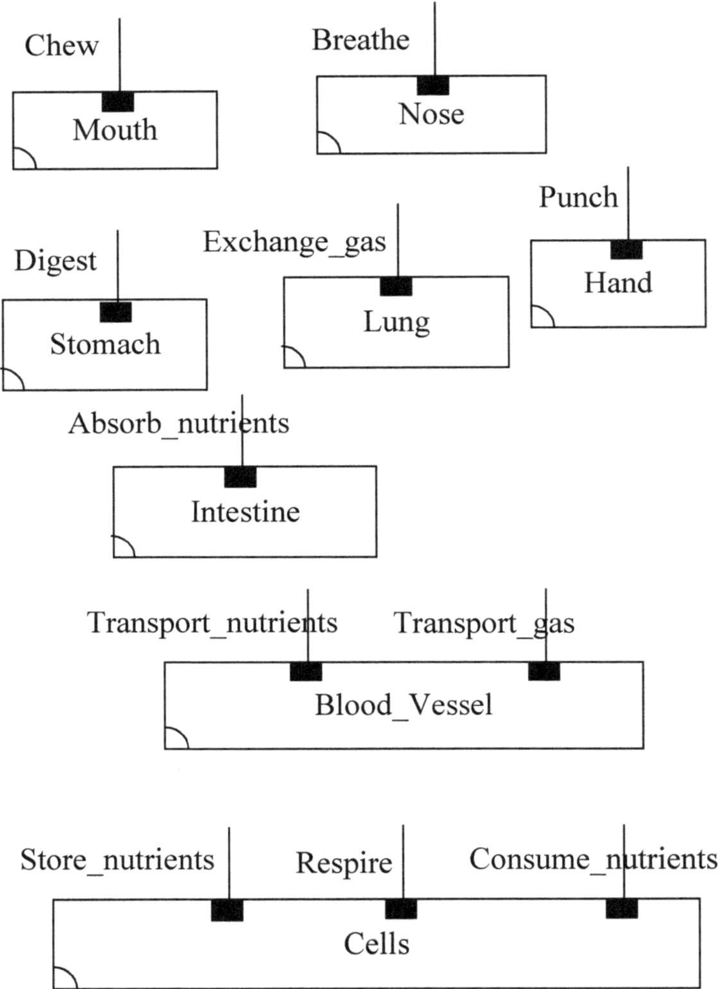

Figure 8-3 COD of the *Human Body*

7-3 Interaction Flow Diagram

The overall behavior of the *human body* includes three individual behaviors: *Eating*, *Respiring* and *Combating*. Each individual behavior is described and represented by an execution path. Knowledge representation 2.0 uses an IFD to describe and represent each one of these execution paths.

Figure 8-4 shows an IFD of the *Eating* behavior. First, actor *Restaurant* interacts with the *Mouth* component through the *Chew* operation call interaction. Second, component *Mouth* interacts with the *Stomach* component through the *Digest* operation call interaction. Third, component *Stomach* interacts with the *Intestine* component through the *Absorb_nutrients* operation call interaction. Fourth, component *Intestine* interacts with the *Blood_Vessel* component through the *Transport_nutrients* operation call interaction. Finally, component *Blood_Vessel* interacts with the *Cells* component through the *Store_nutrients* operation call interaction.

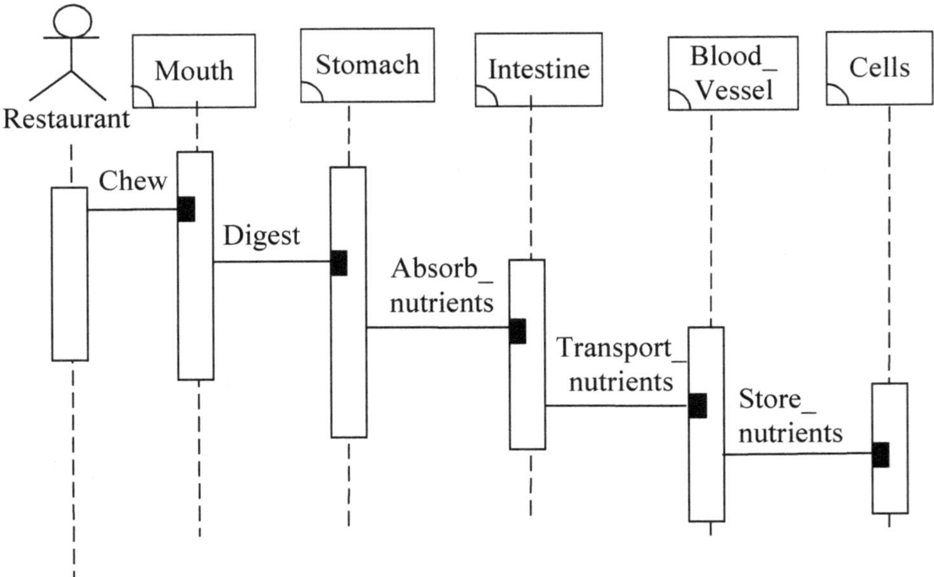

Figure 8-4 IFD of the *Eating* Behavior

Figure 8-5 shows an IFD of the *Respiring* behavior. First, actor *Park* interacts with the *Nose* component through the *Breathe* operation call interaction. Second, component *Nose* interacts with the *Lung* component through the *Exchange_gas* operation call interaction. Third, component *Lung* interacts with the *Blood_Vessel* component through the *Transport_gas* operation call interaction. Finally, component *Blood_Vessel* interacts with the *Cells* component through the *Respire* operation call interaction.

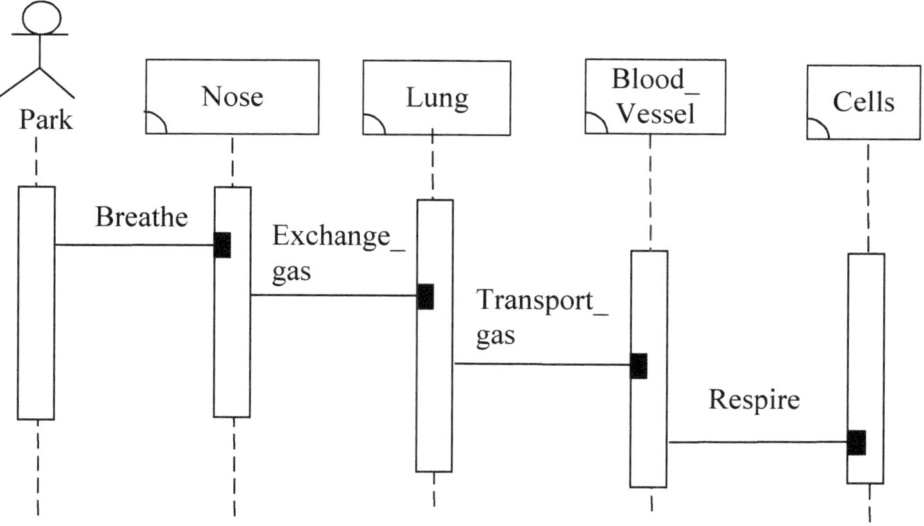

Figure 8-5 IFD of the *Respiring* Behavior

Figure 8-6 shows an IFD of the *Combating* behavior. First, actor *Opponent* interacts with the *Hand* component through the *Punch* operation call interaction. Finally, component *Hand* interacts with the component *Cells* through the *Consume_nutrients* operation call interaction.

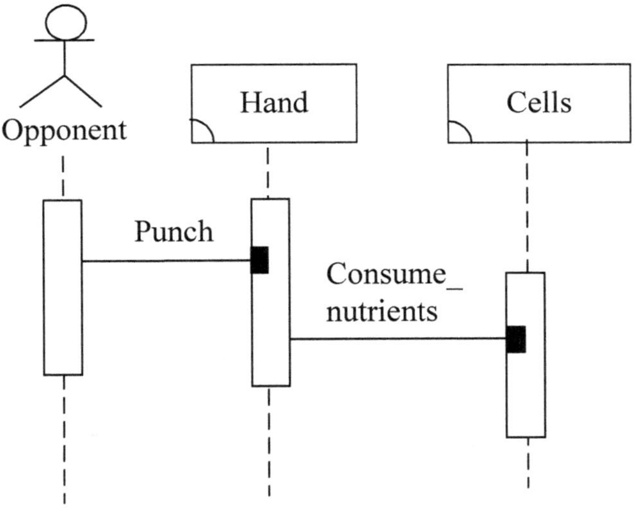

Figure 8-6 IFD of the *Combating* Behavior

APPENDIX A: KNOWLEDGE REPRESENTATION 2.0

(1) Framework Diagram

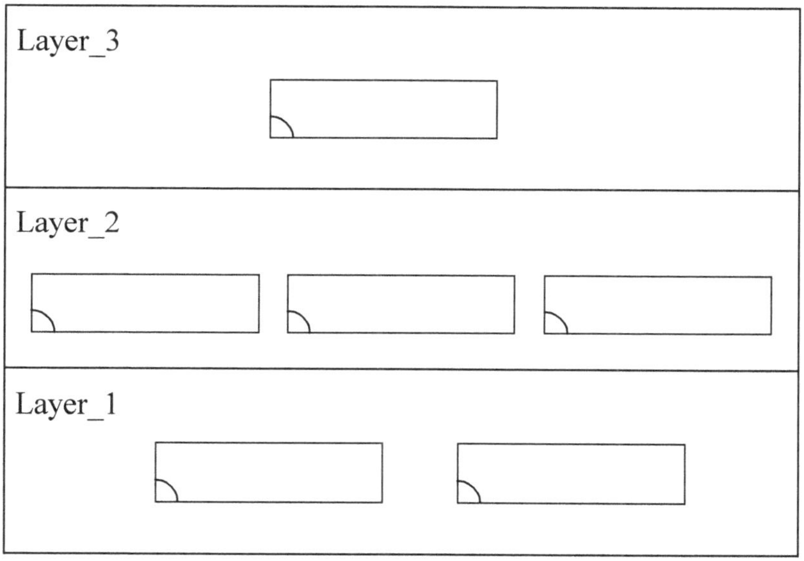

Layer_3

Layer_2

Layer_1

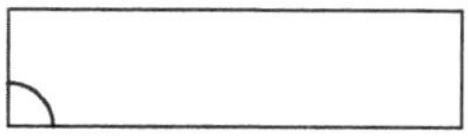

: Component

(2) Component Operation Diagram

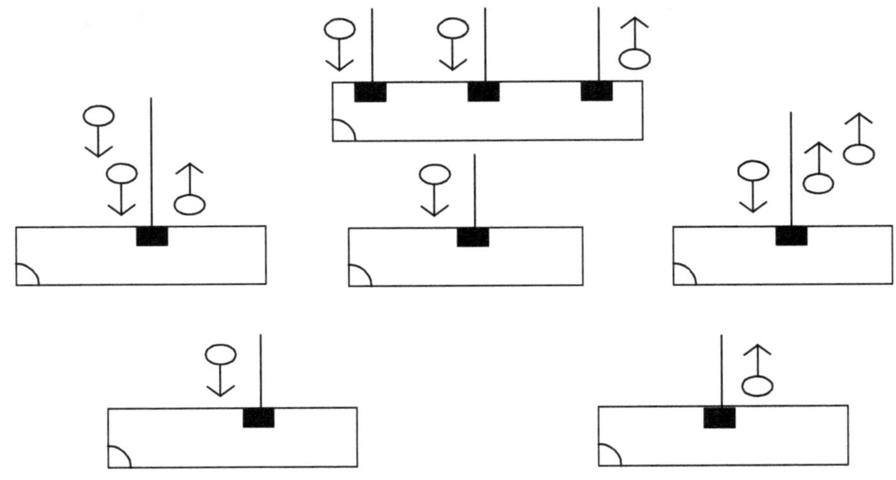

: Operation

: Input Data

: Output Data

: Component

(3) Interaction Flow Diagram

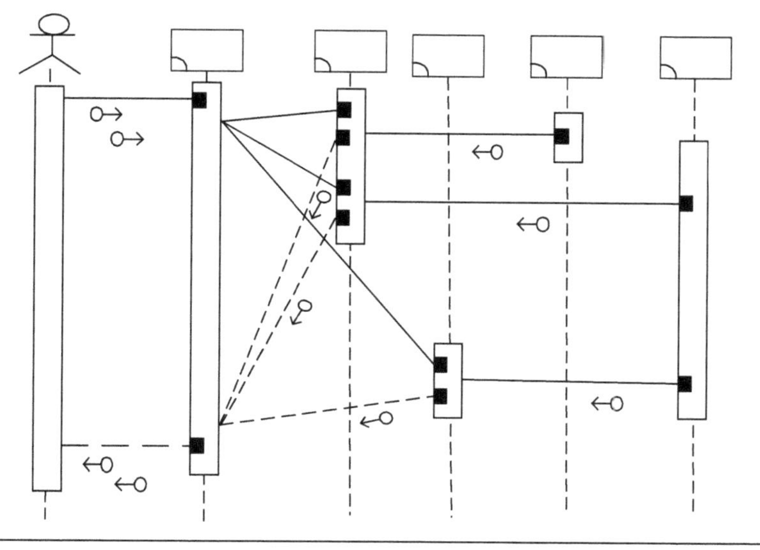

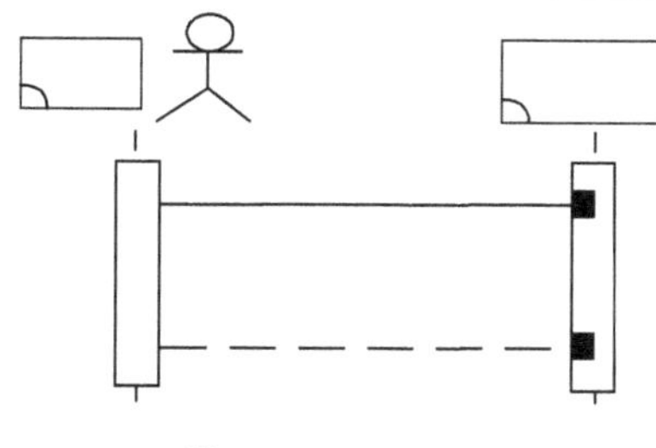

: Operation Call Interaction

: Operation Return Interaction

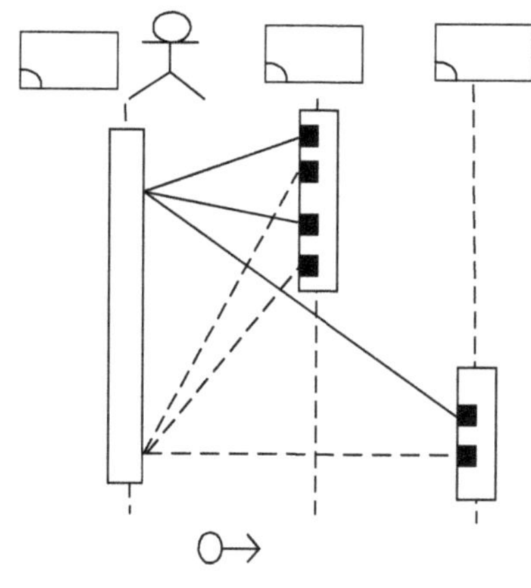

: Conditional Operation Call Interaction

: Conditional Operation Return Interaction

O→ : Input Data

←O : Output Data

APPENDIX B: SBC PROCESS ALGEBRA

(1) Operation-Based Single-Queue SBC Process Algebra

(1) <System> ::= "**fix**(" <Process_Variable> "="<IFD> "• " <Process_Variable>
{"+" <IFD> " • " <Process_Variable>} ")"

(2) <IFD> ::= <Type_1_Interaction> {"• " <Type_1_Or_2_Interaction>}

(3) <Type_1_Or_2_Interaction> ::= <Type_1_Interaction>

| <Type_2_Interaction>

(2) Operation-Based Multi-Queue SBC Process Algebra

(1) <System> ::= <FixIFD> {"|| " <FixIFD>}

(2) <FixIFD> ::= "**fix**(" <Process_Variable>"="<IFD>
"•" <Process_Variable> ")"

(3) <IFD> ::= <Type_1_Interaction> {"• " Type_1_Or_2_Interaction>}

(4) <Type_1_Or_2_Interaction> ::= <Type_1_Interaction>

| <Type_2_Interaction>

(3) Operation-Based Infinite-Queue SBC Process Algebra

(1) <System> ::= "! ("<IFD> " • " *STOP* ")" {"|| ! (" <IFD> " • " *STOP* ")"}

(2) <IFD> ::= <Type_1_Interaction> {"• " <Type_1_Or_2_Interaction>}

(3) <Type_1_Or_2_Interaction> ::= <Type_1_Interaction>

| <Type_2_Interaction>

BIBLIOGRAPHY

[Chao14a] Chao, W. S., *Systems Thingking 2.0: Architectural Thinking Using the SBC Architecture Description Language*, CreateSpace Independent Publishing Platform, 2014.

[Chao14b] Chao, W. S., *General Systems Theory 2.0: General Architectural Theory Using the SBC Architecture*, CreateSpace Independent Publishing Platform, 2014.

[Chao14c] Chao, W. S., *Systems Modeling and Architecting: Structure-Behavior Coalescence for Systems Architecture*, CreateSpace Independent Publishing Platform, 2014.

[Chao15a] Chao, W. S., *Theoretical Foundations of Structure-Behavior Coalescence*, CreateSpace Independent Publishing Platform, 2015.

[Chao15b] Chao, W. S., *Variants of Interaction Flow Diagrams*, CreateSpace Independent Publishing Platform, 2015.

[Chao15c] Chao, W. S., *A Process Algebra For Systems Architecture: The Structure-Behavior Coalescence Approach*, CreateSpace Independent Publishing Platform, 2015.

[Chao15d] Chao, W. S., *An Observation Congruence Model For Systems Architecture: The Structure-Behavior Coalescence Approach*, CreateSpace Independent Publishing Platform, 2015.

[Chao15e] Chao, W. S., *Variants of SBC Process Algebra: The Structure-Behavior Coalescence Approach*, CreateSpace Independent Publishing Platform, 2015.

[Chao17a] Chao, W. S., *Channel-Based Single-Queue SBC Process Algebra For Systems Definition: General Architectural Theory at Work*, CreateSpace Independent Publishing Platform, 2017.

[Chao17b] Chao, W. S., *Channel-Based Multi-Queue SBC Process Algebra For Systems Definition: General Architectural Theory at Work*, CreateSpace Independent Publishing Platform, 2017.

[Chao17c] Chao, W. S., *Channel-Based Infinite-Queue SBC Process Algebra For Systems Definition: General Architectural Theory at Work*, CreateSpace Independent Publishing Platform, 2017.

[Chao17d] Chao, W. S., *Operation-Based Single-Queue SBC Process Algebra For Systems Definition: General Architectural Theory at Work*, CreateSpace Independent Publishing Platform, 2017.

[Chao17e] Chao, W. S., *Operation-Based Multi-Queue SBC Process Algebra For Systems Definition: Unification of Systems Structure and Systems Behavior*, CreateSpace Independent Publishing Platform, 2017.

[Chao17f] Chao, W. S., *Operation-Based Infinite-Queue SBC Process Algebra For Systems Definition: Unification of Systems Structure and Systems Behavior*, CreateSpace Independent

Publishing Platform, 2017.

[Date03] Date, C. J., *An Introduction to Database Systems*, 8th Edition, Addison Wesley, 2003.

[Denn08] Dennis, A. et al., *Systems Analysis and Design*, 4th Edition, Wiley, 2008.

[Dori95] Dori, D., "Object-Process Analysis: Maintaining the Balance between System Structure and Behavior," *Journal of Logic and Computation* 5(2), pp.227-249, 1995.

[Dori02] Dori, D., *Object-Process Methodology: A Holistic Systems Paradigm*, Springer Verlag, New York, 2002.

[Dori16] Dori, D., *Model-Based Systems Engineering with OPM and SysML*, Springer Verlag, New York, 2016.

[Elma10] Elmasri, R., *Fundamentals of Database Systems*, 6th Edition, Addison Wesley, 2010.

[Ghar11] Gharajedaghi, J., *Systems Thinking: Managing Chaos and Complexity: A Platform for Designing Business Architecture*, Morgan Kaufmann, 2011.

[Hoar85] Hoare, C. A. R., *Communicating Sequential Processes*, Prentice-Hall, 1985.

[Hoff10] Hoffer, J. A., et al., *Modern Systems Analysis and Design*, Prentice Hall, 6th Edition, 2010.

[Kend10] Kendall, K. et al., *Systems Analysis and Design*, 8th Edition, Prentice Hall, 2010.

[Mich11] Michaelson, G., *An Introduction to Functional Programming Through Lambda Calculus*, Dover Publications, 2011.

[Miln89] Milner, R., *Communication and Concurrency*, Prentice-Hall, 1989.

[Miln99] Milner, R., *Communicating and Mobile Systems: the π-Calculus*, 1st Edition, Cambridge University Press, 1999.

[Mins74] Minsky, M. L., *A framework for representing knowledge*, Massachusetts Institute of Technology A.I. Laboratory, 1974.

[Pele00] Peleg, M. et al., "The Model Multiplicity Problem: Experimenting with Real-Time Specification Methods". *IEEE Tran. on Software Engineering*. 26 (8), pp. 742–759, 2000.

[Prat00] Pratt, T. W. et al., *Programming Languages: Design and Implementation*, 4th Edition, Prentice Hall 2000.

[Pres09] Pressman, R. S., *Software Engineering: A Practitioner's Approach*, 7th Edition, McGraw-Hill, 2009.

[Scho10] Scholl, C., *Functional Decomposition with Applications to FPGA Synthesis*, Springer, 2010.

[Seth96] Sethi, R., *Programming Languages: Concepts and Constructs*, 2nd Edition, Addison-Wesley, 1996.

[Shel11] Shelly, G. B., et al., *Systems Analysis and Design*, 9th Edition, Course Technology, 2011.

[Smul95] Smullyan, R. M., *First-Order Logic*, Dover Publications, 1995.

[Sode03] Soderborg, N.R. et al., "OPM-based Definitions and Operational Templates," *Communications of the ACM* 46(10), pp. 67-72, 2003.

[Somm06] Sommerville, I., *Software Engineering*, 8th Edition, Addison-Wesley, 2006.

[Sowa91] Sowa, J., *Principles of Semantic Networks: Explorations in the Representation of Knowledge*, Morgan Kaufmann Pub, 1991.

INDEX

N

O

P

S

www.ingramcontent.com/pod-product-compliance
Lightning Source LLC
Chambersburg PA
CBHW060201060326
40690CB00018B/4197
* 9 7 8 1 5 2 2 9 3 0 8 1 5 *